# Road Comic

**Heartbreak, Triumph,
and Obsession on the
Comedy Circuit**

**Barry Friedman**

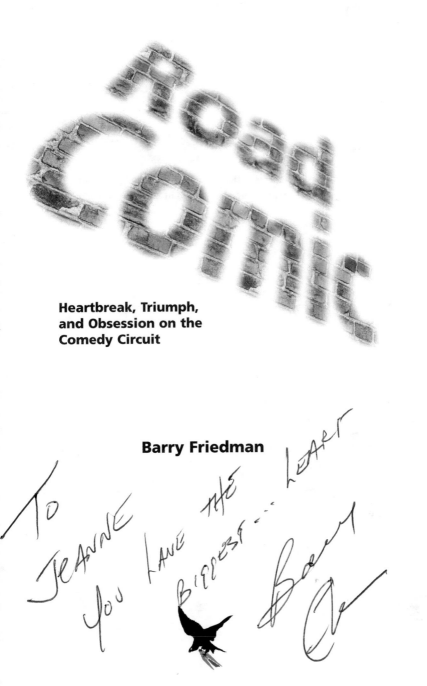

To Jeanne
You have the biggest... heart

Barry

HAWK Publishing : TULSA

Published in the United States by HAWK Publishing Group.

HAWK and colophon are trademarks belonging to the HAWK Publishing Group.

Printed in the United States of America.

LIBRARY OF CONGRESS CATALOGING IN PUBLICATION DATA
    Friedman, Barry
        Road Comic/Barry Friedman—HAWK Publishing ed.
        p.  cm.
        ISBN 1-930709-36-6
        1.Oklahoma
        I. Title
        [PS3563.I42145R4 2000]
    813'.54     80-52413
    CIP

HAWK Publishing web address: www.hawkpub.com

H987654321

*For Paul and Nina.*

*For my mother too, who, I have on good authority, is sitting on a white, puffy cloud and just waiting to send down thunderbolts to burn the asses of people who annoy her.*

# TABLE OF CONTENTS

## Thanks to most of you

 asked a lawyer I dated once whether she wanted her name changed in the following pages. "Nah, I don't care," she answered. "None of my friends read." This came a few weeks before she went into treatment for alcohol, drug, and sexual addiction, so I probably should have asked her again when she got better. She did say, though, "Keep in mind, not everyone else will be so easy."

I don't know if she meant the double entendre or not.

With that in mind, some of the names have been changed; some haven't. My kids, for example, are my kids—Paul and Nina. Whom would I be fooling if I named them Bianca and Hans? As for the others, I changed some of their identities and occupations and residences, if for no other reason than to make their lawsuits easier to defend.

I do, however, want to thank a few people by name: My father for his good humor, bombast, the thousands of dollars he gave me at the Keno pits in Las Vegas and Atlantic City, and for once saying, "Don't try to figure out women. They have funny little minds"; my brother, Wayne, for keeping the sibling rivalry to a minimum, for padding his expense account whenever I was around, and for the hundred bucks he gave me for my high school prom, which I still haven't paid back; my sister, Susan, for taking such good care of our mom while she was dying and for always making sure our dad had a local AOL access number; Ed and Anita, the happiest married couple I know, my aunt and uncle, a perfect aunt and uncle, who let me move in on two occasions, who never let me take myself too seriously (even when I insisted), and who always had me over for Sunday dinners (even when I forgot to bring Anita's cherry danish); Dave, for 26 years of laughs and friendship, for finding the place on the south shore of Long Island that served twenty-five cent pizza, and for that glorious afternoon at Vet Stadium in Philadelphia when we talked of television pilots, ate expensive hotdogs, and laughed at the shirtless fat guy in cut-offs; Ronnie and Louis, the second happiest couple I know, and their daughter, Jill, for being generous, patient, encouraging, trusting me with the hamburgers, and for always having plenty of diet soda in the garage freezer; Marc Glick for your work here and for keeping the international film rights in the unlikely event this is ever made into a movie and distributed to Cuban multiplexes; Charles Viracola for the bad jokes at the Silver Legacy; Vern and Lisa, the third happiest couple I know, for believing in each other, marriage, and God—even when, it seemed, He didn't believe in them; Doug, Mike, and Jan for letting me in the group and for arguing with the woman at dinner who insisted that Jews controlled popular culture; Linda for being my Elaine Benes and for whatever the fuck that chicken dish was you used to make me; Kelli and Christina for letting me read you these chapters even when you knew I was just trying to show off; Shelly for being what every man wants in a woman and a friend as beautiful as you; and Bridget for coming to the MGM the night before she broke up with her boyfriend and for holding my dad's hand by the Bellagio waterfall after my mom died.

Thanks, too, to Lori, Shawna, Amy, Erin, Jenny, Ronnie, Katie, Liz, Daria, Suzanne, another Erin, Kim, Dee, Elena from Russia, the girl at the Etta James concert in Birmingham, another Kim, Leslie, Cindy, Danielle, Deby, Trish, Denise, Tong, Sheri, Tiffany, Julia, and Emmy for the rose, the diet Pepsi and the promise of cold pizza in the elevator at the Excalibur.

There's Bettina, who still deserves an explanation and an apology.

To all the girls who left me standing in hotel lobbies or airport terminals waiting for them to arrive, I want to thank you, too, for the humility, even though I still don't think it would have killed you to pick up the phone to say you weren't coming.

Finally, for those of you who wanted in the book, you're here; for those who didn't, too bad, you're here anyway. Call my lawyer if you got a problem. She's out of treatment.

There's Claudia for reasons that are obvious and Karen for reasons that aren't.

And there's Roxani for reasons I probably won't figure out until the next book.

When Mark McGuire hit his 62nd homerun against the Cubs, the game was stopped and a microphone was set up on the pitcher's mound so he could address the crowd. The first thing he did was to thank his "great ex-wife" for bringing their son to the game. I remember thinking that there were probably millions of divorced men all over the country, screaming at their TV sets, "Oh, yeah, that's the first person I would thank if I broke Roger Maris' record."

Be that as it may, and before I get started, I want to say something to my ex-wife: Jane, you were right. I *was* the Alan Alda character from *Crimes and Misdemeanors*. This too: You deserved better.

Finally, I want to thank those of you who saw me on stage. This is as much for and because of you as anyone.

# Not that you asked

efore becoming a comedian, I never imagined myself having a rational discussion with a woman who had a pierced clitoris; before becoming a comedian, I wouldn't have auditioned to be a French waiter in a movie with "Weird" Al Yankovic; before becoming a comedian, I didn't know that the tears rolling down a beautiful woman's face can be tricky little fuckers; before becoming a comedian, I hadn't had sex with a virgin, bisexual woman, beauty pageant winner, lesbian, or, for that matter, a woman with a pierced clitoris; before becoming a comedian, I didn't think about losing my hair, my mother dying, or troubled German girls I loved in the early stages of ovarian cancer; before becoming a comedian, I never felt the need to separate photo albums into different boxes in different parts of the house; and before becoming a comedian, I never thought about my marriage breaking up, my son hating me, or my daughter with breasts.

What happened once I became a comedian is what follows.

Admittedly, this is just my side of the story. If you want to know what my ex-wife; Miss America; the various club owners and booking agents; the German girl with "bad things" inside her; the Texas girl with the affinity for the pink candle; the curious roommates naked on my bed at the Maxim Hotel; the Paramount paralegals; the girl in the college sorority in Florida; the woman in the laundry room in Redondo Beach; the accident-prone chemist; and all the wonders and weirdoes I've met both on stage and off think about all this, you'll have to wait for them to write their stories.

Even when we're working, comedians can spend up to 23 hours a day doing nothing more taxing than trying to get porn on an Embassy

Suite's *Spectravision*; consequently, we have too much time for self-reflection. I first thought about becoming a comedian while driving home on Interstate 44 in Tulsa after winning $100 at an amateur comedy contest at a hamburger restaurant with jokes about vagina sizes and peeing in a lake. I'm not sure when I thought about stopping, but it may have been while driving on Tropicana in Las Vegas with the entertainment director of the Riviera Hotel and hearing how he didn't think I was funny enough; or it could have been at my home club, which I had worked for years, that had my name on the marquee as *Berry* Friedman; or it could have been in the Bahamas, when, after headlining a club at the Atlantis Hotel, I found myself standing on a bridge with an 18-year-old high school student from York, Pennsylvania with my hand down her pants and wondering if my life (not to mention my hand) was really where it should have been.

Harry Chapin, in his song "Greyhound," said, "It has to be the going, not the getting there, that's good."

I'm not sure how much of it was good, and whether I got anywhere, but here's the trip.

## CHAPTER 1

# Seminal in Seminole

bout 90 miles south and west of Tulsa, Oklahoma, on Route 377 off the Turner Turnpike, is Seminole, Oklahoma. The name *Seminole* is of Indian origin, having something to do with the tribes that moved from Florida to Oklahoma, but to me, when I hear the word, I think potluck dinners, bumper stickers that read *"They can take my gun from me when they can pry my cold, dead fingers from it,"* and oddly named convenience stores with misspelled portable signs in the parking lot. I am in Seminole to do comedy in an Elks Lodge, of all places. These people, the Elks, were the movers and shakers of a town that seems to do precious little of either. They are car dealers, videocassette distributors, oil rig operators, and real estate sales people. They are not investment advisors, bistro owners, and romance novelists. Their names are Big Jay, J.D., Jodee, and Maxine, and it seems like all their male children are named Tyler. They don't drive yellow SUVs or convertible Cabriolets, they mean the Pledge of Allegiance when they say it, they prefer Rush Limbaugh to National Public Radio, they believe in prayer in public school and hunting season with similar ferocity, and they tell racist jokes with abandon and aplomb.

Seminole is the perfect place for sociologists and comedians—as long as neither stays too long.

So, it is here, at the Seminole Elks Lodge, that I have been sent by a local booking agent to do comedy. There are two of us performing. I'm the first act, and I'm making 100 dollars for my 20 or 25 minutes. The other comic, Jed Kirk, will close the show, and probably make twice that for twice as much time. He also said he'd drive, which was good, because as strange as it sounds coming from a road comic, I hated driving. I could never shake the thought of thrown pistons at four in the morning on a Tennessee country road, the sleep-deprived truckers, the Dick and Perry wannabes, and the disgruntled highway patrolman whose girlfriend blew a comic at a corporate gig.

Jed is in his 50's, has a sweet, large wife with whom he travels, and an act from the middle of the 20th century. He still does Gabby Hayes and Akim Tamirov impersonations, for Christ's sake. He works for FedEx, does comedy for a hobby, and is a good friend of the agent, who books him in many of these types of gigs because he's the cleanest comic around. If Kirk's ever said "shit" on stage, it's because he'd lost a bet.

There was a buffet dinner before the show and a DJ had been hired to play country music. Before Jed and I did our sets, the Elks came on stage and told jokes. Jews were depicted as unscrupulous, but sharp businessmen; blacks were shiftless, but rhythmic; Italians were dumb but good cooks with cute accents; and Poles were hopeless morons but inept and jovial. One joke went like this:

"How do you annoy a black? Hide his food stamps under his work boots."

It got the biggest laugh of the night.

The booking agent told me to work as cleanly as possible, which I did, but what do you make of a town where the word *nigger* is acceptable while the word *fuck* is offensive? (The word *cunt* is usually off limits no matter where you go, but words like *fuck* and *shit* are negotiable. Once, in a club in Victoria, Texas, the manager told me not to say *God damn* on stage, but said nothing to the other comic who, when talking about fighters getting into the ring with Mike Tyson for two million dollars, said "For two million, I'd suck Mike Tyson's cock. For three million, I'd swallow.")

I figured these people in Seminole had never seen a Jew, and if they had, didn't like him. I also figured these were the kind of people who drank too much, raised ignorant kids who they dressed in fatigues, found documentary value in *Deliverance*, picked their teeth with the edges of matchbook covers, and generally were, as Randy Newman said in *Good Ole Boys*, the kind of people who didn't *know their ass from a hole in the ground*.

Still, there was a charm here: a Thornton Wilder's *Our Town* without the poetic narrative. Members of the Elks Lodge, while proud of their facility, were jealous of the Masons' larger facility across town. Big Jay weighs 350 pounds but wears striped shirts with the swagger of a man half his weight. Charlene, his wife, worries about his smoking, drinking, and appetite, but told me she'd rather have him happy than thin, so she doesn't nag. J.D., Jodee's dad, works in the oil field outside of town, and begins most of his stories with, "Oh, okay, okay, so this ole boy..."

It was Saturday night in Seminole and if I was uncomfortable in their world, that was my problem. These people were home and, judging as best I could, happy. They didn't need me doing a running commentary of their lives. They weren't on display for me to dissect; all they wanted from me was to do my little jokes and shut up during George Jones.

I had only been in comedy a year or so, so my act didn't have much dexterity. I wasn't good enough to figure out what they found funny. I opened with:

*Okay, so I was behind a bus that had a sign that read, "Caution, school bus may come to a complete stop when unloading children." May? What do you mean may? Where I come from, we don't leave that decision up to the bus driver. We kind of take the ambiguity out of the whole stopping business. And then I went into a restroom and saw a sign on the towel dispenser which read, "Do not insert head into towel loop as it may cause serious injury." Are you having trouble with this kind of behavior? It seems to me, if you insert your head in a towel loop, you deserve what's coming to you.*

The Elks just stared at me. I reassured myself that it was the word *ambiguity* that gave them the problem in the first joke and that some of those towel loops look pretty inviting in the second. Never in my arrogance did I think the jokes just sucked. It got a little better from there. They liked my bit about the escaped inmates hired to work the state fair and my Archie Bunker impersonation as Rhett Butler in *Gone with the Wind.*

> *Ah, jeez, Scarlet, what are you telling me? You're in love with a guy named Ashley? Don't you know that Ashley is some commie, pinko fag? I got two things to say to you there, little girl. I don't give a damn and get the hell away from me!*

I closed with a few old jokes, which I never do. It was a long 25 minutes. I got off stage to a smattering of applause, got a Diet Coke at the makeshift bar, and sat down to watch Jed. I noticed no one was looking at me after my set. There were no nods of approval, no thumbs up, nothing—not a good sign.

Jed, to his credit, knew what the Elks wanted. He recreated scenes from old western movies, did jokes about Jimmy Carter's *lust in my heart* admission, called back to jokes that the Elks had told before we performed, and then, incredibly, did a version of Red Skelton's reading and dissection of the Pledge of Allegiance in which he talks about the inevitable sadness that will develop when liberals, in the name of inclusion and a desire to extract religion from society, remove the words *under God.* Some of the Elks actually cried during this bit; most stood and applauded when it was over.

(Years later, in Vegas, after Bellagio opened their 100 million dollar art exhibit, I was working the Maxim with a comedian who said that in an effort to compete with the Bellagio, the Maxim had just gone out and purchased two more Red Skelton clown prints to add to its collection.)

Nobody, however, at the Elks Lodge would have thought that funny. After the show, Big Jay, Maxine, and one of the Tylers surrounded Jed as if he *were* Red Skelton.

As I was leaving, J.D. and another Tyler came up to me.

"Don't look so sad, honey," Maxine said to me. "You did real good, too."

Call it kindness or condescension, a victory or defeat, but as I sat with Jed and his sweet, large wife at the McDonald's on the Turner Turnpike after the show, eating a hamburger I would soon be getting sick over, and thinking about my night in Seminole, I called it a draw.

## CHAPTER 2

# "I wanna be kissing on you."

on has been a comic, a club owner, a booker, a used car salesman, an ordained minister, and sometimes a combination of all five at once. And speaking of five, that's how many wives he's had but more about that later. He owns the Laff Spot in north Houston, a name we came up with after he broke away from the Laff Stop, a comedy club that had locations in south Houston and Austin and whose name he was leasing. Don didn't want to spend a lot of money changing the sign out front, buying new letters, etc., so we decided to transpose the *p* and *t*, which not only saved him from buying any new consonants, but also had the added benefit of annoying the piss out of his old partners. I met him at the Comedy Showcase in Pasadena, Texas, in 1990. The Showcase was the kind of club that had to hire off-duty police on Fridays and Saturdays because there were usually four or five walked tabs, a parking lot fist fight, a domestic dispute or two, and, if you were lucky, an actual stabbing.

*You've got everything you need in Houston, don't you? Okay, maybe you could use a few more guys at the intersection selling newspapers and handing out roses. I've discovered that I can have a conversation with any of you in Texas, and even if I have no idea what you're saying, it doesn't matter, because all I have to say is "I heard that" and I'm right back in the conversation . . . A guy from Humble came up to me last night and said, 'you're funny as shit.' Am I supposed to be happy about that? I mean, really, I'm funnier than a pile of shit. Wow, that's great . . . A lot of women think men have no sensitivity, no fem-*

*inine side, but only in Texas will a man come up to you with tears in his eyes and say, "Well, I got me a new truck." I dated a girl here in Houston, but it didn't work out because I didn't know what the hell she was talking about half the time. We were in bed one night and I thought we were about to make love, so I went to unbutton her little nightgown, when she looked at me, took my hands away from the button, and said, "Hey, ain't nothing in there you need" . . . What, am I at the refrigerator looking for a beer?*

"Maybe this isn't your kind of room," Don said the night we met, having noticed the number of people who walked out of the club during my show. "Why don't you come work my place?"

I wasn't around for most of the marriages, but years before his fifth, a girl he was dating called him in Vegas and discovered there was another girl in his room. When she confronted him when he got home, Don didn't deny it; he said, "Look, I'm just going to need a *Get out of Jail Free* card on this one." There was another time when he and this same girl were in bed at 2AM when his cell phone, which he had buried in a bag in the closet, started to ring. It was the number he gave out to girls when he didn't want them calling his home number. He didn't move, hoping his girlfriend wouldn't hear the chirping coming from the closet. "Hey, Don," she finally said, "It's sounds like the *Bat Phone*." One time I told him that I read a survey that indicated that the average man sleeps with seven women in a lifetime, to which he responded, "Seven women? That's a bad quarter." On stage, he has a great bit about being married five times. He says the pastor looked at the woman, looked at Don, and said, "Not you again?"

Once, he was visiting his dying father in a Massachusetts hospital, when a nurse came into the room. After she left, Don asked his aunt why the woman looked familiar.

"She was your first wife," the aunt told him.

"How do you forget something like that?" I asked.

"Hey, it was a long time ago."

Don once told me he really couldn't remember which story went with which ex-wife, but there was one incident that involved a wife, her divorce attorney and Don in the attorney's office. Don said that unless the payments were lowered, two of the three wouldn't be leaving the office alive. When another marriage was about to end, Don got a legal pad and told that wife to list everything she wanted. He figured whatever she wrote down would be cheaper than what an attorney would get for her. Apparently, it was. There was another marriage that ended less than a year after it started, but Don took solace from the fact that her parents paid for the honeymoon. "Sounds like a victory to me," I said. I'm not even sure what wife he was on when I asked him how one of his marriages was going. "Hey," he said, "it's going about as well as these things can go." Between wife four and five, he was dating a girl quite a bit younger than he. He liked her and thought perhaps he should marry her, but he wanted to be sure. "You know, she's got very little baggage, so I'm thinking if I brought her to my accountant, he'd tell me she was a good risk."

"But, Don, you're not supposed to bring girls you're thinking of marrying to your accountant."

"When you've been married five times you do."

"You love her?" I asked.

"She gets the job done," he said proudly.

"Marry someone you can't live without," he told me once, "not just someone you *want* to live with."

And he must have done that. He met Patty, his fifth wife, at the Maxim Hotel gift shop. She may have been the best thing to ever come out of the place.

Patty had been married once before, and one day on her way to work, she saw her ex-husband slumped over in his truck. The guy was supposed to pick up their daughter, but didn't show, so Patty was annoyed as she left for work. And that's when she saw him in his truck, slumped over his steering wheel. When she got to work, she called Don and told him the story.

"Well, did you call somebody?" Don asked.

"Like who?" Patty asked.

"I don't know," Don said, "like an ambulance."

"No, fuck him. He's an asshole. He was probably drunk."

"Patty, listen to me. You should have called somebody."

"Why?"

"Look, let's put it this way. If you ever see me even a little pale, you call somebody. I don't care how fucking angry you are at me, if I even sneeze a couple of times, I want you calling a doctor."

I worked with a number of married comedians through the years. Some were faithful, some weren't, and some were but didn't want to be. Some, as the joke went, couldn't get laid in a woman's prison with a fist full of pardons. I don't know if it was a friend of mine, Mike, who teaches theatre, or George Bernard Shaw, who didn't (and this would be the writer, not the CNN anchor), who said, "Ninety percent of virtue is lack of opportunity." My old girlfriend, Yvette, told me that men shouldn't get credit for fidelity unless they're faced with an actual proposition.

"So, unless a woman is in my hotel room, naked, begging me to fuck her, I don't get points for being faithful if I don't?" I asked.

"No. The woman shouldn't be there to begin with."

"What is this, ninth grade algebra? I have to show my work. I got the right answer. Isn't that enough?"

#!!°?)*%#*!( • ?#

I remember after a Saturday-night show once in Overland, Kansas, the headliner and I, a waitress named Brandy, and a few club people went to a bar near the club. The headliner asked Brandy to come back to the condo.

"You're married, aren't you?" Brandy asked and tapped his wedding band.

"No," he said, "I'm not." He winked at me.

"What about the ring?" she asked. "I'm not an idiot!"

Debatable.

"I only wear this so women won't hit on *me*," the comic told her.

"Nuh-uh!" Brandy countered.

"There has to be two tiers in hell," I told the comic. "Men go to one level for cheating on their wives; they go to a deeper level for denying they have them."

#!!°?)*%#*!( • ?#

I met my wife in 1976 in the pantry of a dinner theatre in Tulsa, Oklahoma. I was playing Big Jules from *Guys and Dolls*; she was a waitress, making extra money for the holidays. I followed her into the club's kitchen one night as she was putting away a tub of okra. I asked her what okra was; she asked me what I was doing in the kitchen.

"You remind me of Carole Kane, from *Hester Street*," I said, biting a piece of fried green something that I had plucked from her tray. I immediately felt like vomiting.

She stormed out. I found out years later she thought I said Carole *King*. I put the half-eaten ball of fried green grease back in the tray and thought, *What could I have possibly said that pissed her off so much?*

It was the first of many times I asked myself that.

We lived together for 18 months, and when we decided to get married, we had to find someone to officiate the ceremony who would neither offend my mother who, at the thought of her son marrying a non-Jew, might do a rendition of Dustin Hoffman swinging the cross at the end of *The Graduate*, yelling "*Barry!*" or Jane's dad, whose parched sense of humor might prevent him from missing the humor in having to pay for a wedding between his Methodist daughter and a younger Jew in the first place. I picked a Presbyterian minister because I heard, like Episcopalians, they had none of the dour guilt of Catholics nor the belief that I, as a Jew, was personally responsible for the death of

Christ. No one, not Jane, me, my parents, Jane's parents, the rabbi in town, or even the fat minister himself, was happy with a service that contained music by Prokofiev, vows by Shakespeare, piano playing from my friend Doug, and liturgy from the unoffending portions of both the Jewish and Christian bibles. Jane's dad had the best line of the day when he said, "God himself would be confused as to what the hell was going on in that service."

(Years later, he told Jane that he never knew what the hell I was talking about on stage, which was odd, because he had never seen me perform—not that he would have anyway. I liked him, though; the whole family, too, especially her oldest brother, who once said, "Barry, I love you like a brother . . . in law.")

Jane and I then spent a year in Florida, where I got thrown out of acting school for being difficult and opinionated; then three years in New York City, where I pursued acting; then two in Tulsa, where I wrote advertising; one in Fayetteville, Arkansas, where I did the same; and then two more in Tulsa, where I was a freelance copywriter. After that, I began doing comedy. Jane and I were driving on Interstate 44 in Tulsa when Jane saw a message board advertising a comedy contest at a local club. First prize was 100 dollars.

"Why don't you try it?" she asked. She would rue the day she ever asked.

I won the contest.

The first comedy club I ever worked was the Tulsa Comedy Company. The owner of the club, Jerry Pippin, was in a comedy duo with a guy named Bobby Sessions—*Pippin and Sessions*. Bobby was the bald one with something like seven fingers (the other three having been lost in a bar, a prison, and the gears of a wood lathe). Jerry was the straight man, paid the bills, and tried to keep Bobby away from cheap alcohol and bad women (or maybe it was the other way around). Jerry's girlfriend/wife (no one knew for sure) was a woman named Robin, who had lost her leg to cancer. Jerry must have had a soft spot for people with missing appendages and digits. Robin helped book Pippin and Sessions, which was difficult because they weren't very good; more importantly, Bobby couldn't always be found. Bobby did impersonations, but he drank too much, too, so he didn't always do the voice of whom he said he would be doing. And even when he did, the voices all came out sounding like a tired Elvis. In addition, Jerry's timing was often off and he couldn't always remember how the jokes went; still, there was something endearing about the two of them on stage.

One of Jerry's funniest jokes was his take on meeting Robin:

"I drove up, saw her, and said, "Hey, babe. *Hop* in."

Amateur Night in Tulsa was on Tuesday. It's sometimes called Open Mike Night or, as I once heard, No Talent Night. It's where new comics would be allowed to perform for 5 minutes or so. In most clubs, this night is held before the regular week of shows, which is usually Tuesday or Wednesday through Saturday or Sunday. During the regular shows, a club would book a headliner, who would do 45 minutes; a feature, who would do 30; and an opening act, who would do 15. In Los Angeles and New York City, most of the clubs were showcase venues, which meant up to fifteen professional comedians would be scheduled for 15-minute sets. It was almost impossible for amateurs to work these showcase rooms; that's why the road clubs were so important. Only away from New York and Los Angeles could a comic get regular stage exposure. There was a club in New York that did schedule a show for just new comedians, but it was held at 5PM, and the comic had to bring in four paying guests before he was allowed on stage.

Open-mikers are an odd collection of working opening acts, drunk college students, angry 30-somethings with career frustrations, smug radio disc jockeys, and young magicians, guitar acts, and hypnotists without much skill. My favorite in Tulsa was a woman who dressed as a nurse and spoke in rhymes about anal sex and catheter insertions.

The first time I worked the club in Tulsa, I was the eleventh comic performing. Jerry told me to do six minutes, to make sure I got off stage when I saw the red light over the door, to not say *fuck* too much, and to tell the emcee what I wanted for an intro. The host for an amateur night was usually the best local comedian or a working comic who happened to be in town. It was the emcee's job to bring up the other comics, announce their credits (which usually consisted of the generic "He works clubs, colleges, please welcome . . .") and do time in between the acts.

I had no comedy credits.

"Please welcome a copywriter, and a guy who's never been on stage before, Barry Friedman, " said the emcee, a magician with a bad toupee and an unkempt goatee, who lived in a camper outside the club. (A few weeks later I walked by his camper and overheard him telling some girl, "Tell me you love me. Tell me you love me!")

I came on stage and threw three dollars to the people in the front row. "I don't know how funny you'll find me," I said, "so I thought this might help."

It was the first thing I ever said on stage; it was the first time I ever heard laughs from people who paid a cover charge.

I questioned if there were any other reason Oklahomans went to the lake except to pee (*It would kill you people to use a bathroom*); I described Jane's desire to go through natural childbirth (*Problem was . . . she couldn't deliver the baby without the use of drugs*); I did an impersonation of Archie Bunker in *The Wizard of Oz* (*Ah, jeez d'ere, little girl, get away from the curtain!*); I talked about the difference between men and women (*Women don't compare their private parts the way men do. You'll never hear one woman say to another, Hey, Carol, I've got a vagina THIS big*); and complained about my high school prom date (*She was a born-again Christian. But she wasn't always one. She had fucked every guy in high school; I ask her out and she finds the Lord*).

I ended the show by tossing the audience a few more dollars. As I walked back to the alcove where the other comics for the evening stood, paced, and reviewed their notes, a woman with the upper right side of her teeth missing came up to me and said, "You're cute. I really wanna be kissing on you."

Jerry said "good job" and told me to come back the following week.

As I left the club that night, Bobby Sessions was doing a guest set . . . by himself. He was impersonating a highway flagman, his three remaining fingers wrapped around the microphone stand.

"I can hold up traffic for fucking miles if I want."

It was funny; it was depressing.

For the first six months, comedy was just a hobby. I worked Tuesday nights as often as possible, and from time to time, Jerry got work for some of the local comics and me around town at bars, corporate parties, and, occasionally, at the club. Jerry would give us 50 dollars for these gigs, maybe 150 dollars for the opening slot at the club. He'd make the same or more for himself in commissions, but none of the comics I knew complained. We were getting paid to tell jokes. Soon, Bobby was back in rehab, Robin disappeared, and the club closed and was replaced by a *Suds and Duds*.

(I saw Jerry years later in Las Vegas. I was working the Maxim; he had gotten a job on a talk radio station. It seemed odd. He didn't mention—and I didn't ask—about Bobby, but I'm sure he still owed Jerry money.)

On stage back then, I'd do material that I had been practicing the week leading up to Open Mike night. These are bits I thought about while driving, while showering, while eating dinner. Comedy was becoming the most important part of my life. I'm pretty sure Jane saw it as a hobby out of control.

"What kind of man would pursue this kind of life?" she asked a friend of ours. "The kind you divorce," was the reply.

In the movie *Crimes and Misdemeanors*, there's a character, played by Alan Alda, who's the subject of a documentary film. He is a windbag—self-righteous, self-important, and self-consciously cute. In the movie, there's also a rabbi who's going blind, an ophthalmologist who gets away with murder, and a young engaged couple (the girl is the rabbi's daughter). At the end of the movie, all the characters somehow come together for the wedding. I looked over during this scene and saw Jane crying.

"Why are you crying?" I asked.

"Because these two kids have no idea what marriage is about; no idea how all their dreams will change and how it's never going to be what they expect."

"That's not why you cry," I said. "You cry because the one guy got away with murder and you cry because the rabbi, who was a saint, is too blind to see his own daughter get married. That's the injustice; that's the crime; that's the reason, if you're going to cry at all, you cry."

"Well, of course you wouldn't cry. You're the Alan Alda character."

In Jane's defense, I don't think she ever thought I was funny. It's tough enough being married to a comedian; God knows what it's like to be married to one who doesn't make you laugh and doesn't make a lot of money. As the years went on, it was clear to both of us that the world thought I was funnier than she did.

In the spring of '89, my advertising work started drying up, so I started taking more comedy work—even though it would only pay $75 or $100 per night when I could get it. Jane would tell you that I didn't pursue the ad work hard enough, that comedy was a self-fulfilling prophecy, but as I said earlier, it's my book, so you get my version of events. One night, in our kitchen, I leaned against the refrigerator and told her, "I'm sorry about the money, the lifestyle, how things worked out. But don't you ever want to just forget for a night? I mean, eat ice cream in bed, make love, and throw pillows at one another? We used to be good at that. We can fight again in the morning."

As I was saying it, I thought, *This is a nice speech I'm giving.*

"I'm too angry," she said.

#!!°?)*%#*!( • ?#

The first road gig I ever did was in a Holiday Inn in Omaha, Nebraska, an eight-hour drive from Tulsa.

Petey Gruber, another local Tulsa comic, and I were asked by Jerry to go and perform four shows in two nights. The hotel management didn't turn the room, which meant that since the crowd wouldn't be leaving, the two of us would have to do two different shows per night. Usually an audience has better things to do than stick around to see the same comedians twice in one night, but apparently not in Omaha. I was to do thirty minutes up front; Petey would do an hour. Neither of us had enough material to do one show of that length, let alone two, but Jerry told us, "Just fuck around with the audience and talk slower if you have to."

I got $125 for the four weekend shows; Petey $150. (Jerry probably made $200 himself.) We would both get our own room at the hotel, and if we got there early enough on Friday, we could eat free at the happy hour buffet. The management also had a special deal with a Perkins nearby. Comics got a 25 percent discount on all food except the specials. Petey drove, and made me sign a waiver releasing him of any liability should I be injured in an accident. It was a needless request, for the only thing that could have killed us on the trip was boredom.

My grandfather, a cab driver in New York City for 40 years, used to tell me that when driving by a cemetery to always turn down the radio as a show of respect for the dead. Kansas has a lot of cemeteries; the radio was off most of the trip.

The club at the Holiday Inn, a meeting room primarily used for Kiwanis luncheons and Rotary meetings, was half-filled on Friday, slightly busier on Saturday. Petey struggled so much, the first night he asked everyone in the room what he or she did for a living, once even having the following exchange:

"So, what do you do?" he asked a guy in a striped shirt in the front row.

"I'm a salesman."

"So," Petey said after a momentary delay, "you sell things, huh?"

I did every joke I had ever written, did in fact talk slower, and chided the crowd for not having more of a life.

*You ever think to yourself, I asked the crowd, sitting here at an airport hotel in Omaha, Nebraska, watching the same comedian do the same jokes that something, somewhere went terribly wrong?*

I was told by a number of people that evening that I should have been the headliner. It was the first but not the last time I longed to hear that. Jerry told me once that all opening acts think they're funny enough to feature; all feature acts think they should be headlining; and all headliners think they're underpaid.

During the drive home, I knew I wanted to be a comedian full-time. I just didn't know if I was funny enough and, more importantly, didn't know how to tell Jane.

A friend of mine told me, in front of Jane, that if I was going to do comedy, I had to keep the checkbook full and my dick in my pants.

I tried to do both; I did neither. The money just wasn't there. As for the other, it's more complicated—or maybe I just want to believe that. Even after we both knew the marriage was going to end, I still wanted to stay faithful; an absent father perhaps, a less than perfect husband, certainly, but I thought keeping my dick in my pants was a worthwhile goal. It's a bad cliché about being able to look at yourself in the mirror, but once a marriage begins to evaporate, the mirror is no longer an ally; it's better used for looking at the reflection of naked waitresses. And when that happens, infidelity loses its mystique, and is easier to commit. And when it becomes easy, it becomes understandable—at least to the one cheating. Jane once told me that there were lots of ways to have an affair without actually having sex. And I had lots of them.

I don't know what Jane thought of all this, but one time, over dinner, she asked if I was faithful.

"Yes," I told her. And, at that point, I was.

"You mean you never even got a blowjob in a parking lot somewhere after a show?"

The way she asked made me think it was another disappointment she was prepared to live with.

Actually, the first blowjob I got outside the marriage was from a girl who worked for the red cross. You don't forget the first time your cock's in the mouth of woman it shouldn't be. I met her at the Fifth Season Inn at one of those one-niters. She was heckling me during the show, so I stopped, and said to her from stage, "Listen, you keep this up, you won't get me in bed."

"Oh, yes, I will," she said.

She blew me in a handicapped space in the Fifth Season parking lot. As the top of her head disappeared into my lap and I saw my unbuckled pants around my calves, I knew I had become a different person. I also knew that if Jane were ever in a car with a half-dressed out of town salesman, I would deserve it. On the way home, I promised myself that I would never tell Jane and never do it again.

I kept one of those promises.

Years later, at the same Fifth Season Hotel, right after my divorce, I met a girl, Dee, who had beautiful shoulders and teeth, tiny hazel eyes, tattoos of grape vines on her back, an absolutely perfect ass and, as it turned out, an extensive soft-core pornography collection. We spent the night together at her apartment, but—and this is important to the story—didn't fuck. We maybe spoke two or three times after that. About a month later, Jane called to tell me she was getting obscene phone calls from some girl who said she knew me. It took me a few days to figure out it was Dee, so I called her to find out if she was making the calls.

When I started out in comedy, I always used the outgoing message on my answering machine to show people how funny I was—or at least to try. My message at the time I knew Dee was a rambling, transitional digressive monologue about being home, but maybe not, but even if I wasn't, there was a big dog watching the place, etc. Anyway, Dee admitted that, yes, she had called Jane, but not to scare her, but just to let her know what a great fuck I was and how, after spending the weekend with me in New Jersey, she couldn't walk for a week.

"But, Dee, we were never in Jersey."

"Oh, no?"

"Yeah, I'm pretty sure of it. We were in Fort Smith . . . Arkansas. Not even close to Jersey."

"Barry, don't deny it."

This went on for a few minutes, until I said, "You know, Dee, even if we had been in Jersey, we didn't fuck. And even if we did, I'm not that good at it to make you sore for a week."

Days later, Jane got another call from Dee. When I called Dee to ask, plead with her to stop, I got her answering machine.

*Hi, this is Dee. I'm not here. Oh, wait, yes, I am, and besides, even if I'm not—and I am—I have a big dog. Woof woof! In fact, my name's not even Dee; it's Jane.*

Neither Jane nor I heard from Dee after that. I imagine she met another comedian with a better message.

I also auditioned for *UHF* around this time, which "Weird" Al Yankovic was directing. Originally, I tried out for the part of a French waiter, but since I don't know how to do a French accent, the producers gave me another, and as it turned out, bigger, role. I had three lines:

*I left the report on your desk, sir.*
*Yesterday, before you left, sir.*
*Yeah.*

All right, Hyman Roth's Cuban Hotel scene with Michael Corleone in *Godfather II*, it's not, but it was a feature film.

*I was in the major motion picture, UHF. Anyone see it?* (Usually one or two people would raise their hands). *Oh, good, thanks for the*

*support. At least you got to go in one car. Anyway, you know how*
*most movies wind up at a dollar theatre; UHF opened at a dollar the-*
*atre. And then it came out on video, but only on Beta.*

Interestingly, Michael Richards and Fran Drescher were in *UHF*,
too. Obviously, all our careers soared afterwards.

I also kept a journal through this time in which I write of my
ambivalence about marriage, sex and comedy. Jane found it, though, on
my computer and read an entry where I talked about how close I had
come to sleeping with an engineering major from Texas Tech.

"But I didn't. That's the point," I told Jane.

"But you wanted to. That's *my* point!"

In a rare display of candor, I said, "I want to sleep with ninety percent of the women I meet, but I don't."

Apparently nobody wants that much honesty.

She said that comedy was an irresponsible career for a grown man
with two children and couldn't understand why a man would prefer
telling dick jokes in a bar to spending time with his family.

She was right. Thing was, I hated leaving, but loved going. It was
another one of those distinctions that only I appreciated.

Then, one Sunday in early 1992, while I played the Trump Castle in
Atlantic City, Jane called and said it was over. She knew it years before
when she was pregnant with Nina. Jane said the thought of getting
older and raising two children essentially alone, spending weekend
after weekend with no money and no husband, she decided there was
going to be more to her life. She said I could have prevented this from
happening. (She asked me many times to do something else, anything
else: radio sales, insurance sales, once, even selling ladies' handbags in
Texas. I always refused—until the end, but by then she wasn't asking
anymore, and, in retrospect, I only offered because I knew she wouldn't
accept.)

And, yes, she had met somebody else, but that's not why the marriage ended.

*My ex-wife told me there were three things she wanted from me: to respect her, to listen to her, and, let's see . . . hmmm, something else.*

I was in Houston, working the Laff Stop, and staying at the Allen Park Inn, a place I always seem to be when the women in my life get feisty, when Jane called to say we were no longer married. She said that she and Bob—the guy she was seeing—brought our separation agreement to court, and after the divorce was granted, went to lunch.

"You went to lunch?" I asked.

"Yeah, is there a problem?"

"You don't go to lunch with your boyfriend straight from divorce court."

"You don't?"

"No, you go home, sit on the sofa, open a box of Kleenex, watch *Sally*, and call your friends to bitch about what a prick I was and how you wasted good years of your life with me."

"You're unbelievable," she said. "It's all a movie to you, isn't it?"

As for me, I spent the night with a girl who had two kinds of vibrators—one for her clitoris, one for her vagina.

We all get over divorce differently.

Months later, while watching the kids at the house (this is when Jane and I were still getting along enough to do things like this), I found two letters we had written each other after I was thrown out of graduate school. In her letter, she was sweet and vulnerable; in mine, I was characteristically breezy and self-conscious. I loved the girl in her letter.

She happened to come in while I was on the floor reading.

"You see these?" I asked, motioning to the letters.

"Yeah. You want them?"

"That's not the point. What do you think of the two of us?"

"*I* sound like a sniveling, scared little girl. *You* sound the same."

I hated when she talked in italics.

"I liked this girl a lot," I said, motioning to the box.

"Yeah, well, I don't. I was a floor mat for a lot of years."

#!!°?)*%#*!( • ?#

Years later, I noticed a picture I had taken sitting on the new coffee table in the house she now shared with Bob. Jane, beautiful, troubled and very unhappy, was sitting between our kids and trying to smile. Nina, who was three, was in her lap, and Paul, who was eight, and wearing a blue tank top and looking bored, stood with his arm draped around Jane's shoulder. Only Jane was looking at the camera, and at me, who was taking the picture. She told me later she couldn't understand why I insisted on taking the picture instead of being in it. Why was I more comfortable as an observer than a participant? Looking at the picture years later, I still didn't have an answer.

A word about Bob: Even though he moved in ten days after the divorce and married Jane a short time later, he wasn't the reason for the divorce—no matter how I characterize him on stage. They met, she says, at a Cub Scouts meeting (Bob was a volunteer scoutmaster, I think; Jane had signed Paul up), but I remember Bob from the comedy club. He used to come by himself; he told me once he loved comedy.

"My wife, too," I said sarcastically.

I don't know if in fact that's how they met, but I do know Bob provided Jane and the kids with a number of gifts, including a coat that looked like a mink (I never got that close) and an SUV.

Remembering the blowjobs I got in Rapid City, Fresno, Amarillo, and Wichita during the same time, I figured she was entitled. The months of our separation were an elixir for her: she was vibrant, alive, and wildly sexy. *I* would have had an affair with her. A few weeks before the divorce, I asked if she wanted to stay married. Had you seen her reaction, you would have thought someone told her she looked like Carol King.

A rabbi told me that it would be difficult for a woman to get "air time" in my life; when I asked Jane if that were true, she said, "Sometimes just walking into a restaurant with you takes too much energy."

This, too: At Paul's first Little League baseball game—and this was a month before our divorce—I had to work in Houston, but I wanted to see the first few innings of his game.

First time up, Paul struck out on three awful-looking swings.

"I hope you're happy," Jane said.

"What are you talking about? Why would I be happy?"

"Maybe if you were around more, and could have practiced with him, instead of doing comedy in bars, he wouldn't have struck out."

"Do you sit up nights thinking of ways to tear my heart out or does this come naturally to you? First of all, comedy is what I do for a living. Second, I *do* work with him. Besides, you never saw me play baseball. I couldn't hit a low fastball either. "

A good line, but this wasn't the time for good lines.

The next time up, Paul closed his eyes, swung as hard as he could, hit a line drive over the shortstop's head, and didn't stop running until he reached third. As he was running, I was too: down the first base side, around the backstop, all the way waving my hands and throwing kisses. He returned them after he reached third with a stand-up triple. I looked back and saw Jane, arms folded, shaking her head in disgust at my overt display of affection. As I returned to her side of the field, I picked up my bags and asked, "Do I get credit for that at bat?"

At Paul's little league awards banquet later that year—and after weeks of taking him to the batting cage—he won "Most Improved Player" on his team at the year-end team barbecue. Jane made a point of thanking his coach.

The world changes when you have an ex-wife in it.

CHAPTER 3

# Ants & Elephants

once knew a Miss America who loved bookstores, drinking Coca-Cola straight from the two-liter bottle, eating peach Pull-n-Peel licorice, and for about 11 weeks during the winter of 1996, me. I always promised her I'd keep this story to myself, but after awhile, you forget why you make the promises you do. And, anyway, I'd like the story even if I wasn't in it.

Miss America conjures up thoughts of a girl in a one-piece bathing suit and high heels who gives a speech offering to use her title to bring love to the world and not one of a girl whose panties and faxed love letters you have in a large photography box in your closet. I didn't even know Asia was Miss America until she sent me a packet of photos of herself in her winning banner and tiara. There were other pictures, too, some of her partially nude, some in just jeans and a t-shirt, and some in leotards as she led middle-aged women in an aerobics or step class. She captioned each one with thoughts ranging from *Reach for the Stars!* To *I love you* to *I want you to fuck me in the ass.* "If you ever get on *Oprah!*," she said, "these will be the proof that you slept with a Miss America." When I asked her why she would send me a photo of her in a tiara with the caption *Reach for the Stars* (the ones about anal sex I understood), she told me that when she was in the Miss America Pageant, it was the only greeting the girls were allowed to write on their official pageant photos. Pageant organizers feared, she said, that if she wrote something innocent like *Love, Asia* on the photo, some lunatic would conclude she was ready to hop in his El Camino and join him on his ostrich farm in Elko, Nevada. Asia then told me about the creepy Japanese businessmen in the audience who invited her back to Kyoto; the homesick, crying contestants who were her roommates in the shitty hotels, and the ultimate winning of the title.

"When were you going to tell me you were Miss America?" I asked.

"You mean I didn't tell you?"

"Believe me, *that* I would have remembered."

I met Asia when she was a 17-year-old, 6'1" Arizona high school senior. She was the most beautiful girl I had ever seen—certainly the most beautiful who has ever loved me or, incidentally, who's ever met me at an airport in a blonde wig. She hung out in bookstores, art museums, and enjoyed walking around university campuses, too, as if she needed any more going for her. Girls like Asia get by in life just fine without library cards or season subscriptions to the opera. But, at that time, I was 33 years old and married enough to know that I shouldn't be flirting with a 17-year-old high school student, regardless of how gorgeous or well-read she was. I first saw her in Tucson during a show at a club that was in back of a Chinese restaurant. I don't remember the name of it, but I do remember being able to smell egg rolls and beef from stage. The first time I worked there, Asia was sitting in the front row with her boyfriend. I must have worked that club six, seven times in the late '80s, early '90s, and whenever I did, Asia would come to the shows— sometimes with her boyfriend, sometimes without. Sometimes we would go over to the restaurant and eat dumplings and fried noodles and dip them in duck sauce. I found out she was a model (not that I couldn't have figured that out on my own). I had done some modeling as well, but while I was doing Brunswick Bowling ads in Tulsa, Asia was modeling Armani tops on the cover of the Italian edition of *Elle*.

Asia and I started going to lunch, alone, and from time to time I'd meet her at her modeling agency during the day, where I'd usually find her in the make-up room, trying on different shades of lipstick, or sitting behind the reception desk, reading Kipling, or even in her manager's office, complaining about her pictures, weight, or modeling schedule. We'd eat at a small Italian restaurant across the street and she'd tell me about her bald, lazy, verbally abusive boyfriend and I would tell her dirty jokes and draw pictures of Fred Flinstone on her napkin. Pretty harmless stuff—unless you consider the choreography going on in my head. Once, over a meatball parmesan hero, I gave her a copy of Joan Didion's *The White Album* and *Slouching Towards Bethlehem*, explained in some detail why Vienna Fingers were better than Oreos, and then told her a joke I first heard on *Hill Street Blues*. Frank Furillo had lost a promotion due to some minor snafu in the police department, when his girlfriend, Joyce Davenport, asked him how he felt. It is then Furillo told her:

*"An ant and an elephant spend the night making love. It's beautiful. But the ant awakes the following morning and discovers the elephant has died. 'Damn,' says the ant, 'one night of passion and I've got to spend the rest of my life digging a grave.'"*

It's my second favorite joke.

Asia took a drink from her Diet Coke, pulled a strand of hair away from her mouth, and said, "I've never heard anything so sad and funny at the same time. If I were the ant, I think it'd be worth it."

She got it.

Some lunches can be more erotic than sex. I wanted to kiss her that day, standing in the rain and in the parking lot, but I didn't. She was practicing the joke over and over because she wanted to make sure she had the proper irony and sadness in her voice when delivering the *It was beautiful* line. I could tell you it was somewhere between her telling me that joke and the fighting over who got to keep the leftover meatball sandwich and her saying, "You always make me smile, Barry," that I knew I would love her someday, but I don't remember.

I do know that six years later, when the man she was living with stopped making love to her and I was divorced and working a club in Houston, Asia came to my hotel at the Allan Park Inn and laughed and cried and left her cell phone on while I undressed her. Maybe I remember more than I forget. She came to Jacksonville, Florida, a month after the day in Houston, and met me in a blond wig at the airport. We then spent the next three days driving around town in a small rental car, watching R-rated movies on the *Spice* Channel, eating peach licorice, drinking Diet Coke, and listening to Natalie Merchant on a cheap Walkman. I could have told her about love then, on the day when we went to St. Augustine and she sat on a $17^{th}$ century cannon and sucked on a lollipop; or could have told her after I came off stage one night and saw her smiling and eating stale popcorn in a corner booth; or could have told her at the airport when she said she'd move in with me if I asked.

But I didn't.

It's easy falling in love with a woman who gets the joke; it's just not as easy knowing when to tell them. Of course women like Asia almost always know anyway.

Months later, after that trip to Jacksonville, after she stopped sending me notes and tearsheets of her on magazine covers and calendars, and her panties in a brown envelope with a pair of red-tipped scissors, after we stopped having phone sex while she drove on the interstates in Texas and I paced my kitchen floor in Tulsa, after I sent her a copy of Didion's *After Henry* and my own homemade greeting card listing her as my favorite model, I sent her a copy of my favorite joke.

> *A guy hears a knock at the door. When he opens it, he discovers a snail. He picks up the snail and throws it as far as he can and shuts the door. Three years later the same guy hears a knock on the door. He opens it and discovers it's the same snail.*
>
> *The snail looks up at him and says, "What the fuck was that all about?"*

I never found out if she got it, though.

CHAPTER 4

# "I'm still sore from the D & C"

ell, it's a long story, but my name is Star, as in, you know, a star in the sky."

I just asked her name; that was all. And I couldn't imagine what the long story was about, but figured if I was stupid enough to ask a stripper her name, I deserved an answer like that. Most strippers have stage names (I guess because the name *Windy* sounds more erotic than, say, *Phyllis*), so I was pretty sure she wasn't born a Star, but it was possible. We were both in Hastings, Nebraska, at the Baby O!, a club in a prefab aluminum building off a county road. It was a Tuesday night in February and Star, along with three other girls, Cinnamon, Brandy, and Tammy, would be stripping; I, along with a 345-pound middle act, who called himself Tiny Bill, would be doing comedy.

Not that it was strange for comedians to work the same clubs as strippers, but it was unusual to do so on the same night. And I would have complained to the agent about it, a guy named Ken Muller out of Sioux City, Iowa, but I wasn't funny enough to bitch about anything and, besides, there were always more comics than clubs. When I first started working the road, I'd work places like these all over Oklahoma, Arkansas, Texas, Kansas, Iowa, Mississippi, and Nebraska; clubs that would have nights devoted to karaoke, strippers, comedians, wet t-shirts, and $1 shots. In the mid '80s, it seemed like every city with a hotel and a lounge had a comedy night, so I figured this night was just part of the landscape, figuratively and literally. I remember actually thinking of that line while eating a half-priced hamburger at the club— *part of the landscape, both figuratively and literally*—and was so proud of it, I wrote it down on the edges of a Budweiser coaster. Hastings was on

Tuesday, the first night of the tour: Wednesday was Kearney, Nebraska; Thursday was Norfolk, Nebraska (Johnny Carson's hometown); and then Friday and Saturday were Sioux City, Iowa in a place called Pepperoni's.

I made $125 for doing about 45 minutes; the other comic made $75 for about 30. (I think Ken got $100 for booking the room, which entailed making a phone call.) Before the show started, a bouncer from the Baby O! came on stage, rolled up the girls' dance mat, and introduced Tiny Bill. (After I did *Evening at the Improv* many years later, I was working a show at an Oklahoma City hotel lounge, and a bartender, reading from an index card at the microphone, brought me on stage by saying, "Okay, this next guy's named Barry who did some shit on cable. So, give it up for him ... come on!") In addition to the salary, the clubs always paid for the comedians' accommodations, too—usually a Super 8, Motel 6, or some irresponsibly franchised Best Western and, if lucky, a discount on food if the club had a kitchen. Ken would get a 10 percent agent's commission from Tiny Bill and me, and he'd get it in cash when we arrived in Sioux City.

There were worse ways to make a living. A comic out of Kansas City told a joke about how his father said to him: "You know, son, when I was your age I had a house, a wife, children, responsibilities. Look at you. You run around the country telling jokes, hanging out in bars. What do you have to say for yourself?" The comic thought for a moment, smiled, said, "I don't know. I win."

That was just one of many jokes I wished I had written.

Tiny Bill and I were to go on stage at 10PM. Star and the girls were to dance from 8 to 9:30PM, and then do another set from midnight to 2AM. They were also on a tour, working other small towns in Nebraska and Iowa, though after tonight, we wouldn't be working together.

I arrived at the Baby O! around 8:30PM and saw Star dancing on a small leopard skin rug to an INXS song. She was wearing a black G-string that held the fanned bouquet of the ones and fives given her by men who approached the stage, a light blue bikini top with a rose over one of her breasts, and ankle boots that zipped up the side. Her navel was pierced and she had another small tattoo on her right ankle. There was a bottle of Vaseline Intensive Care by her side, which she used between dances to rub on her hands and knees, and she was dancing underneath a big screen television, which was tuned to a Cubs-Reds game from Riverfront. Seeing the lotion reminded me of a night in southern Kansas a few years earlier when I performed at a club that had booked female Jell-O wrestlers the previous night.

"I mean, I think I got all the shit off the stage," the manager told me, "but you may want to be careful just in case. That stuff is slippery."

Years later, when my brother was getting married, I took him to a topless club in Glendale, California on Thanksgiving Night, 1997, for his bachelor party. One girl, completely nude, stood over him, straddled his head, looked down her legs, and said, "Wayne, I hope this is the last vagina you see that's not on your wife." Later, while doing an inverted push-up that enabled her to thrust her crotch in his face, she told him the benefits of a prenuptial agreement.

"It's a little tough to take financial advice from you right now," I said.

That table dance cost me $40 for my brother; Star was lucky if she made $5 here in Kearney. (A pitcher of beer at the club was also $5 .) As I mentioned, I made $125, after commission; Star and the girls got $200 . , . before tips. Tiny Bill said he heard some guy offer Tammy an extra $25 if she'd blow him in the parking lot.

Back then, my act was an uneven assortment of crude jokes, pedestrian observations about feminine hygiene ads, and Tammy Fay Baker insults, but I had a bit, which I still do, of asking a woman to come onstage and take off her bra through her shirt. Considering what Star and the girls were doing, this bit—you should pardon the pun—fell flat. During the show, I recall a woman in an orange tank top, yelling, "Hot fucking damn!" and Tiny Bill eating ribs throughout, but not much else. I was grateful the club owner had turned off the ball game and surprised that Star stayed for the show instead of joining her friends in the trailer behind the club that acted as their hotel.

After my set, Star held out her hand for me to kiss. "You're funny," she said. I noticed her big, brown eyes, perfect teeth, wide smile, and surprisingly good complexion. You need to spend time in clubs like these to know why that's surprising; need to see what alcohol, stale air, long hours, cigarette smoke, sleeping in a trailer outside the club, dancing in a mismatched G-string and bra, and blowing guys in parking lots can do to a woman.

We sat. "You want a table dance?" she asked.

"No." But I did. I also wanted to fuck her.

Actually, I didn't know if I did, but I assumed she would think I did, and that was enough to make me act like I wanted to. Strippers intimidated me, especially pretty ones with good skin, but there was nothing I could tell her, short of sincerity, that she hadn't already heard from a thousand other guys.

Later, as the girls did their second set, Tiny Bill and I ate cheese sticks, tried to guess how much cash a pair of panties could hold, and wondered which of the girls had lesbian tendencies. By the end of the evening, Star's G-string was overflowing with cash. As we all waited to get paid, Star, the other girls, Tiny, and I sat at the bar and talked about life on the road until 3AM. Tiny Bill and I then went back to the hotel; the girls went back to the trailer. I then called my wife, read Linda Ellerbe's autobiography, and went to bed. I didn't think about Star; I didn't not think about her.

Kearney is about 60 miles from Hastings, so an easy travel day for a comedian. Some gigs are 400 miles apart, so you have to spend the entire day on the road, but for this one, I didn't have to leave Hastings until early afternoon. As I drove out of town, I passed the Baby O! It was even more depressing in the light.

A comic's routine on the road begins with the drive to the new city. Once there, and assuming no car trouble, speeding ticket, or crazed hitchhiker who wouldn't get out when he was supposed to, the comic would find the hotel and club and then a place to eat. You think you'd get tired of hotels with numerals after their names, long drives on state roads past Wal-Mart Superstores and cemeteries, convenience store snacks, tasteless Chinese buffets from restaurants on county health department watch lists, and living out of a suitcase, but you don't—at least not for years. After unpacking, a comic would then make some phone calls, call the club owner to say he had arrived, and then work on his act, read the local paper, or, more likely, take a nap, watch television, find a mall, or see a movie. Shows at bars that did comedy started later than the ones at legitimate comedy clubs, around 10PM, so depending on how bored the comic was from sitting in his room watching *Oprah!*, reruns of *Wings* and *Wheel of Fortune*, he might arrive as early as 8PM and just hang out till show time.

There was nothing subtle about the comedy performed at these one-nighters. It had to be fast and loud. The sound systems were usually inadequate, the lighting was laughable, and help from the management concerning crowd control was non-existent. Often just getting the crowd to shut up was the toughest part of the evening. I knew a comic who played the guitar during his act—well, until he smashed it over the head of some guy who rushed the stage. After shows at clubs like these, a road comic (and most were males) would stand around the bar, waiting to get paid, or hovering around waitresses, waiting to get laid. It was often easier getting the latter.

The hotel in Kearney consisted of bungalow-style cottages with wood slatted doors, flowered bedspreads, and thick, stiff brown shag carpeting. In my room, the air conditioner had created a stain on the wall that looked like the horn of Africa, and the heater, a floor model, had a pilot light, which I was sure would go out in the middle of the night, killing me. To be asphyxiated in a shitty hotel while lying on lousy bedding with MSG-laden Kung Pao Chicken lodged in my intestines was also, I feared, part of the comedy landscape.

I went to a movie.

That night, I was on stage, so I didn't see Star come into the club, but did see Tiny Bill wave his hand in the air, smile, and point towards the door.

"Guess who's here?" he said, as I came off stage.

"Who?"

"Star."

"You're kidding."

"A stripper drove to see a *comedian*?" he asked. "Now that's impressive!"

She was standing at the bar and put her hands up to her face when she saw me.

"Remember me, from last night?"

"Just how many strippers do you think come see me on a regular basis?"

I wish I hadn't called her that.

"You were very nice," she said. "I wanted to see you again. That okay?"

I asked her to breakfast.

We went to a Waffle House by the University of Nebraska-Kearney, where, not that I expect you to believe this, my wife really did go to college for a semester back in the '70s. Star sat with her legs tucked underneath her and ate pancakes—lots of pancakes. *The hungry soul, the hungry heart; and apparently, just hungry, too,* I thought, *a perfect cliché.* I decided against writing this insight down.

"So what are you doing here?" I asked as I stole a piece of rye toast from her plate.

"I thought you were sweet. So many of you comics aren't. I wanted to see if I was wrong."

"I'm married." God, was I smooth.

"I didn't come here to go to bed with you."

God, was I disappointed.

She then told me about her 5-year-old son, Skyler; how she was 15 years old when she had him, how her boyfriend (not the kid's father—that was someone else) beat her, and how her own father, who hated her dancing, bought her a car anyway so she'd be safe when she traveled. She had powdered sugar on her face, ate with her fingers, and gulped her milk. I felt like I was eating breakfast with Jody Foster from *Taxi Driver*.

"You like the way I dance?" She asked.

I looked up. She had a milk mustache.

*Unbelievable.*

"You want to come back with me?" I asked.

As we walked to the room, I made a mental note to remember the number, thinking it would make a great story someday, but it escapes me now. The air was hot and dry and the wall under the air conditioning was more stained than ever when we got inside. A country station was the only thing I could get on the radio that was built inside the television. I kept thinking of that joke about how if you played a country song backwards, you could get your truck, wife, and dog returned to you.

"I'm nervous," she said.

"*You're* nervous!? Why?"

"This is different."

What was different? Was I?

"I can't make love to you," I said, surprising myself. Of course I could.

*You're the Reason God Made Oklahoma* came on the radio.

"Why not?" she asked, as she bit the tip of her index finger.

"For lots of reasons, not the least of which is I'm married."

"I understand," she said.

I didn't think she did, and didn't even know why I was telling her.

. . . *And I'll be missing you,* Shelly West kept harmonizing.

"There's more to it," I said as I sat on those god-awful orchids. "You are every girl I always wanted but never got. You're every cheerleader, every Delta flight attendant, every young housewife in a grocery store produce aisle with a pretty smile. I want this moment, Star. A lot of men would. To be with you in this shitty hotel in the middle of Nebraska with a bad heater is, in a strange way, perfect—absolutely perfect. I just don't know how to fuck a metaphor."

I waited my whole life to say something like that to a girl like this.

She stopped biting her finger, turned over on her back, and flung her head over the side of the bed. I watched the top half of her body disappear. I was looking at her legs.

"I can't make love to you, either," came the voice from the floor. "I just had an abortion last Friday and I'm still sore from the D&C."

Some words are better heard without having to look into the eyes of the person saying them.

I can't explain why, but I pulled her upright and pulled off her t-shirt with the star on the front, kissed the small scar below her right eye, her perfect nipples on breasts that hadn't been filled with silicon or saline. I then took off her pants and shoes, licked across her stomach, and then went down on her. She came twice; she was still wearing socks. She then thanked me for not sticking it in and said most guys would have anyway—"stitches or no stitches."

I can't remember if we watched *Nightline* afterwards or just listened to more country music.

"Can I see you later this week in Sioux City?" she asked as she lay on top of me, gently running her fingers over my face. "We're dancing across the street from Pepperoni's." I grabbed her hand, kissed each one of her fingers, slowly scraping my teeth down the length of each one. I heard her nails inside my mouth.

"No, I don't think that's a good idea. I'm not sure this was a good idea."

I had just made a metaphor come twice in my wife's old college town. There was much that was not good.

"Maybe it would be better if I stayed on my side of town," she said as she bounced from the bed, found her clothes over the heating grate, sat in the brown corduroy chair beneath the Horn of Africa, and got dressed. I loved watching women take off and put on jeans. I didn't want Star to rush getting dressed because I felt like I would never see a girl like this naked again.

It had warmed up some as we walked outside. A bank sign that alternately flashed *11F* and *2:17* illuminated her Pontiac Sunbird, which was dented pretty badly on the front passenger side.

"Does your wife know how lucky she is to have you?" Star asked. She put her arms around my waist, stood on her toes, and kissed me right below my chin and tapped my nose a few times with her middle finger.

"I think my hugging a stripper in a parking lot in Kearney, Nebraska at two o'clock in the morning, after having oral sex, is not something my wife would consider a stroke of good fortune—especially in a place she went to college."

I didn't mean to make a joke, but she didn't laugh anyway. She got into the car her father bought, and would probably fix, waved through the partially defrosted window, and drove away. I hate the sound of tires on gravel; it's an angry sound. I also hate saying good-bye to women in parking lots late at night; they almost never leave happy.

And she did stay on her side of Sioux City.

Years later, in Vegas, a topless dancer with capped teeth, who was sitting in a desk chair in my room at the Maxim Hotel, told me the most popular line men use to pick up strippers is when they ask them out to breakfast.

At least I didn't let Star do that table dance for me.

CHAPTER 5

# Lost year in North Hollywood

n December of '92, three months after my divorce, I met Joan Fagan, a comic, by a bank of elevators at the Riviera Hotel in Las Vegas. Joan was looking to rent her badly furnished condo in North Hollywood; actually, she was looking to rent the badly furnished upstairs loft of her badly furnished condo in North Hollywood. The downstairs was already rented to another comic, who, Joan promised, was hardly ever there.

By that time, Bob had already moved in with Jane. I thought it ironic that the comedian/husband who couldn't provide for her was providing the deed for the house for her and her insurance agent/boyfriend, but nobody asked what I thought—especially not the two of them.

As for me, my friends Ria and David said I could stay at their house after my divorce. The fact that they said this before Jane and I had even separated gave me some idea what my marriage must have looked like. I moved in with them in the summer of '92, and was only planning on staying until the fall, but I was still there when I ran into Joan in Las Vegas.

Ria and David took no money, had their Salvadoran housekeeper do my laundry, bought or made me dinner frequently, made Paul and Nina feel comfortable when they came over, and listened to my stories of the road and the women I met. On that last point, they wouldn't let me have girls over (I think more out of a sense of their own safety than any morality concerns). During this time, Jane and Bob took out an insurance policy on me and named themselves both the owners and the beneficiaries. They got behind on the premiums, though, and when the company called me for payment, I cancelled the policy.

"Sir," the woman from the insurance agency said on the phone, "are you sure you want to leave your loved ones unprotected?"

"I think these loved ones, yeah."

"Barry," David said one evening as he patted out hamburgers in their kitchen, "if you're found dead somewhere, Jane and Bob would have a lot of explaining to do."

"What really hurts," I said, "is they only took out two hundred grand. I'd like to think I was worth more than that." I wasn't.

Meanwhile, when Paul and Nina would come over, we'd go out for pizza, talk about summer trips to the Bahamas or Vegas, drive to the mall and make fun of the yuppies at Abercrombie and Fitch. Then, at night, we'd all pile into the king-sized bed. The kids made sure I slept in the middle, so they could both hear the stories I would tell them—some which were true, some which weren't, and some which had to do with what I would tell their kids someday. Someone told me that if you couldn't do anything else as a parent, you should try to get your kids to smile before they went to bed.

I was still working the road, but I was now playing places like Vegas, Reno, Princeton, the Bahamas, Austin, New Orleans, and Houston instead of Enid, Oklahoma, Chanute, Kansas, and Nagadoches, Texas. I didn't feel as guilty about working the road anymore, either, because I knew that when I'd return, I'd be able to take Paul and Nina to school, to lunch, and generally see to them without having to end the day apologizing to their mother for being a comedian.

When I'd return from a gig, I would sit around the dinner table and tell Ria and David about the women, whackos and wonders I met on the road. I thought I might write a book someday with that title—*Women, whackos, and wonders*, but figured it was both pejorative and redundant. Ria would have copies of e-mails that I had sent her and check off items as I filled in the details of some sordid tryst.

Sometimes late at night, while lying in their spare bedroom, which was more of a storage room, regardless of what they now say, and staring at the ceiling, I realized how parenthetical I had become. I was a novelty for my children and a live-in court jester for my friends. Even in my own life, I felt like a visitor. Maybe *Storage Room* would have been a better title for the book. All my other friends were married, and even though I got most of them in the divorce, I found myself spending most nights by myself—driving around the city, going to dollar movies, bookstores, or to the University of Tulsa, where I'd sit on the library steps and look at the skyline of downtown—and all the time pretending Charlie Rose or Terry Gross was interviewing me. I was alone and lonely.

I needed to move. In terms of comedy, the best place to go was either New York City or Los Angeles. For the kids, the best thing would have been had I stayed in Tulsa and continued doing comedy from there. A dad, even a divorced one in a storage room, is better when he's only two miles away.

So, naturally, I moved . . . on New Year's Eve, 1993.

I could be such a selfish fuck.

That night, I took the kids to dinner at a Chinese buffet, kissed them goodbye in the driveway of their old home with the new stepfather, packed everything I owned in my 1985 Mazda GLC, including a CD Player I got from Jane after a last-minute fight in the driveway, and left Tulsa for southern California and Joan's loft. I drove through the ice in western Oklahoma, the rain in central New Mexico, the heat in all of Arizona, where I didn't stop at the Grand Canyon because I didn't want to go alone, and the outlining towns of Los Angeles, like Industrial and Palmdale—the ones that only Quentin Tarantino seems to know and love.

I heard once that Los Angeles is forty suburbs looking for a city, and when you arrive from the east, you can see why. I drove thirteen hours a day for two days, again talking to myself. I scribbled notes for my act on the back of gas and toll receipts, sang into the rear-view mirror, and rehearsed conversations with women I someday hoped to meet. I arrived on the corner of Bellingham and Magnolia in North Hollywood at around seven on a Sunday night, a few days after New Year's. It's a sobering moment to know that everything you own can fit in the back of a sub-compact; sobering, also, to know that without your stereo speakers, you wouldn't even have to put down the back seat. I had a longer relationship with that Mazda than with any woman I've ever known. New Mexico's a long state, so you have time to think of things like that. Besides, I probably treated the car better.

I found the condo, walked up the stairs, and discovered a room about seven by eighteen feet. This was my new home. There was a chest with a broken bottom drawer, a television, which, upon closer inspection, didn't get all the stations or colors, and a love seat with one cushion missing. It folded out into what could only charitably be called a bed. The loft was sloped, so I couldn't stand up straight in much of it. On the other side of the room, across from the stairs, was a bathroom with a toilet and sink. (The shower was downstairs). A three-foot-high cast iron rail ran the length of the loft, so, obviously, without a wall enclosing the room, I would be able to see and hear everything that went on below; in turn, I would be on display 24 hours a day for any visitors downstairs. The other comic had a separate bedroom, a full bath and shower, which we would share along with the common living area, the kitchen, and the dining room. He was paying Joan $650; I was paying $350. That first night, I plugged in my phone, had two Burger King cheeseburgers for dinner, and fell asleep on a blanket and a pillow I stole from the downstairs couch.

"Dad," Paul called to tell me the next morning. "I'm going to school now, but I just wanted you to know that I cried when you left. Bye."

I told him I did, too, but I don't think he believed me. He was nine at the time. I knew I should have kept him on the phone longer. And even though I hadn't spent even a full day in Los Angeles, I knew it was a mistake leaving him, his sister, and Tulsa.

I wish I had told him that, too.

Comic Richard Lewis said that to be successful in comedy, nothing—not women, children, or ambivalence—should get in the way of that pursuit. But not a day went by for me in comedy where at least one of those things wasn't in the way.

#!!°?)*%#*!( • ?#

Don put it more succinctly. I was working his club during my separation and, before going on stage one night, called Jane to see how the kids were doing. We started arguing and she hung up on me. As I slammed the phone down, Don, who had witnessed the whole thing, said, "What's the matter with you? Don't you know that you never talk to a woman before a show? I don't care if it's your mother, your wife, girlfriend, or daughter. They only bring trouble. I don't even like talking to my female staff before I go on stage."

There's another story about a comedian who was working a cruise, where phone calls can cost as much as $15 per minute. He told his girlfriend, who lived in L.A., that he'd call nonetheless, but he'd have to keep it short. She agrees. So, he does. He calls from the ship an hour before show time, says something like, "Hi, honey, I love you. Hope everything's good, but I gotta go. Remember this is expensive, so bye, I love you," and is just about to hang up, when the girl says, "Fine, be that way." He says, "No, no, honey, it's not that. It's expensive, remember? Fifteen bucks a minute. Plus I have to go on stage" when again she says, "Well, go, if you have to. If that's all you can give me, if that's all this relationship means to you, fine." The story goes that the comic stayed on the phone for 28 minutes, or $420, to prove to his girlfriend that he loved her and wasn't more concerned with comedy than her feelings.

When I moved to L.A., I was seeing a girl, Yvette, whom I had met at the Austin Laff Stop two nights before my divorce. She had asked me to move in with her before I left for Los Angeles, but I turned her down. I told her I had to pursue my career, and to some extent that was true, but mostly it had to do with infidelity—mine. I knew I'd cheat on her eventually and couldn't see living with a girl I knew I'd hurt. I eventually ripped her heart out over a German girl I met in the Bahamas, but on that first morning in North Hollywood, lying on the floor with a Burger King bag under my back, I called Yvette and told her I missed her. I knew then; I know now: She loved me more than I deserved.

I would have been more comfortable in New York, where I grew up, but there are more television and film opportunities in southern California. I had been in comedy five years at this point, and I was making enough of a living not to do anything else, even if I was still driving the Mazda and had only $945 in savings. I wanted to be on television and didn't want to wind up a 50-year-old comic with a bad toupee, performing in a lounge in an Ocala, Florida Holiday Inn. For me, indeed for most comics, the easiest way out of comedy was to get cast in a sitcom. The irony was that most of us wanted on shows we otherwise wouldn't watch. I thought, for example, *Full House* was the most unctuous, predictable, poorly acted show on television, but I would have been a great Joey.

In Los Angeles in the early and mid '90s, comedy was filled with neurotics, alcoholics, divorced men, bitter women (and vice versa), underweight drug addicts, fat Southerners, tall Jews in sweaters, closet homosexuals, repressed heterosexuals—and this doesn't even include the real nuts. This isn't just hyperbole. Comedy attracts malady. There has to be something odd about people who perform. You shouldn't need to have that much acceptance and validation on a nightly basis. Laurence Olivier was asked why he acted; his answer was simple: "Same as everybody else: 'Love me, love me, love me.'"

For a comedian to break into a club, he or she would need some combination of luck, recommendation and talent, though the last wasn't always necessary—look at Paulie Shore and Tom Arnold. Once the person in charge of booking saw a comic and deemed him or her funny enough, the comic could then work the club. It's called being *passed*.

Being passed was no guarantee of work, but it would allow you to get on the schedule. The shows at the city's premier showcase clubs, The Improv and The Comedy Store, would begin around 8 PM and go to one or two in the morning. Each comic would get from 15 to 30 minutes, and if lucky, be able to schedule work in two or three different clubs a night. You'd run into the same comics at these clubs; you'd swap road stories, talk about bookers, money, sex, perhaps even comedy, and then go out to eat at a diner until two or three in the morning. I spent many early mornings on the 405, driving back to the Valley from some club, looking at the passing cars and wondering how many of them had depressed comedians inside who were bitching about stage time or scribbling a new joke on a piece of paper on the dashboard.

*You know all those people in New York City, talking to themselves, screaming at people for no reason. They're not crazy. They're comedians on the way to a gig.*

The problem most comics faced was deciding how much time to stay in Los Angeles or New York, auditioning for movies and television, and how much time to go out and work the road. In Los Angeles, a comic could be seen; on the road, he could make a living. On the road, headliners could make as much as $2000 for the week; the feature between $500–$700; the opening act around $400. There are countless stories about comics who missed out on television and film roles because they were working a cruise or headlining a Funny Bone in Omaha instead of staying in Los Angeles. On weekdays, most of the L.A. clubs paid less than $25 a set, weekends slightly more, so comics had to work the road to make any money at all. Some clubs, in L.A. and New York, didn't pay at all. When I worked The Comedy and Magic Club in Hermosa Beach, all I got was dinner—my choice of a burger or a chicken sandwich. (I once worked with a magician there who kept his pigeons in a cage backstage. As I walked by the pigeons, I swear one of the birds had a look that said "*Help me.*" I'm sure I had the same look.)

There's a joke which goes like this: Two feature acts are talking and one asks, "What did you do today?" and the other replies, "Went to the mall and watched the headliner buy stuff." Air travel was almost never included for any of the acts, but lodging would be at either a hotel or an apartment the club was renting. When I went out on the road during this time, I usually went as a headliner or a feature, except when I worked Las Vegas, and there I went in whatever slot the clubs wanted. In L.A. and New York, comics were looking for nightly slots at these showcase clubs, where, the hope was, they would be seen by a television producer or agent. It didn't matter what slot they worked on the road. No matter how funny a comic is, if he's performing in Amarillo, Texas or a casino in the Mississippi Delta, no one from Paramount will be there to see him and ask him to read for the part of Tom Cruise's brother in *Mission Impossible V.*

Pilot season—that time of year when most television shows are cast—was January, February, and March. Clubs in Los Angeles are overflowing with comics, agents, producers, and casting people. Obviously, it is even more difficult to get stage time during this time of year, which, of course, is when I arrived. On those nights when there was no work at the showcase clubs, I'd spend it working some one-nighter in a bowling alley in Ojai or a corporate gig in Rancho Cucamonga. If there was no work at all, I'd go hang out at the clubs and then wind up going to Jerry's Deli in the Valley watching celebrities eat dinner. I'd then go home to my sloped loft and call my kids, Yvette, or some woman I met on the road and try to talk her into phone sex.

Usually, I'd wind up at The Improv on Melrose. The Improv had locations in Santa Monica, Brea, and Irvine, but Melrose was the main room. Its owners, Budd Friedman and Marc Lono, could often be found at their eight-top in the lounge/restaurant, adjacent to the showroom, where they wined and dined industry people, celebrities, and the hot comic—the *flavor of the month* as he or she was called.

Other comics would eat and drink at this lounge, too, cajoling, bitching, bragging, and whining about their careers, and all the while trying to catch Budd or Marc's eye. While Budd and Marc made the decision on who would work their clubs, it fell to the discretion of others to make the schedule. For a while, Budd's stepson Ross had the job. On Mondays or Tuesdays, comics would call Ross, and he'd dole out the slots for the week. If the comic was approved or had an agent who requested him for an industry showcase, the comic would get stage time. I wasn't the first, didn't have the second, and so wasn't given the third. With no set to do, no hope of performing, I did what most comics did: hung out in the bar.

Eventually, Marc did see my show and told me, "I like the jokes a lot, enjoy the insights, I just don't know how you feel about what you're saying."

I didn't know what you did with criticism like that.

The Improv was also host to A&E's *Evening at the Improv*, perhaps the best-known cable comedy show at the time. Many comics used their appearance on it as a stepping-stone to other television work, but by the time I did it—two installments before it was taken off the air—*Evening at the Improv* was like a prostitute performing her last trick of the evening: tired, past her prime, and just going through the motions. There was no prestige in doing it anymore. Besides, it seemed like every one had already done the show. Don told me that one of his ex-wives had already done the show.

When I finally did it, I wore jeans, a shirt with too many buttons, and a mismatched tie. And while I never slick my hair back, I did that too. I looked like an inept gangster. I don't know what the hell I was thinking. I've never worn that outfit before or since. The jeans were *green*, for Christ's sake. More importantly, all through my set, I felt myself rushing to get to the punch line and skipping over material I didn't think the crowd would like.

My opening joke was about smoking. Usually, the joke was a long set-up, determining who in the audience smoked, what non-smokers thought of them, and then I'd deliver the punch line. On the taping, however, just this:

> *Non-smokers are jealous of smokers. We don't know how we're going to die, but you . . .*

The joke went fine, but delivered too damn fast. *Goddamn It*, I thought through the 8-minute set, *I'm funnier than this*. On other jokes, I forgot words. In one bit, I pull out my Oklahoma driver's license and referred to it, but in listening to the tape, I heard myself say *"Now on the Oklahoma driver's . . ."* I forgot to say the word *license. Fuck!*

#!!°?)*%#*!( • ?#

A woman associated with the show who, parenthetically, had a pierced clitoris, mentioned after the taping that I was one of the few comics who did the show whose act didn't have to be "sweetened" with laughs. In a comedy world filled with few of them, I counted that as a victory. Crystal Bernard was the host that evening, and she was nice enough to send Paul an autographed picture of herself, which he proudly hung on his wall next to 8x10 pictures of Carrot Top, Yogi Berra, and me. This was when he still got excited about things . . . and I was still on the wall.

Ironically, I didn't do *Evening at the Improv* the year I lived in Joan's condo. It was a year later, after I had moved back to Tulsa, that I got the show. The day of the taping, I checked into a hotel a few blocks away and practiced my set in front of a little mirror by the bed. I remember having no one to call before or after the taping. When I walked in to the showroom, the same comics I had seen twelve months earlier were still there, ordering the same pasta dishes, drinking the same bottled water, and still looking at Budd and Marc with the same mix of frustration, expectation, and resignation. Who knows how many years they had been there? And how many more years they would be?

It rained a lot that year I lived in North Hollywood; it was a relentless rain. I guess because there's so little of it, when bad weather comes to southern California, it likes to be noticed. It kept me in the loft much of the time. I didn't have money to go out anyway, didn't know many people, so I watched the city's never-ending parade of local news shows. No wonder Angelinos think the world revolves around them; they turn on the T.V. and all they see are themselves.

I wrote countless letters to friends on a typewriter that vibrated so much on Joan's dining room table that the neighbors below complained. When the rain would let up, I'd walk to a post office down Bellingham, have a slice of pizza at Joe Peep's, and then return home and wait for the phone to ring. I tried to stuff my clothes in the broken chest and bought a futon to replace the mattress in the love seat, but it wrecked my back and knees. A doctor in Van Nuys said my pain was stress-related, but every problem in L.A. is considered stress-related. I assumed the leg would have to be amputated. Day after day, night after night, I found myself lying on ugly bedding, looking at the phone, snapping my fingers as if I could make it ring telepathically, staring at a ceiling I was only partially renting, and asking myself the same questions I asked myself at Ria and David's. Only now I didn't have a wall, closet space, or a television that could get NBC.

And nothing much was happening with my career. I was passed at a few clubs, but didn't get much work. I worked with Bill Hicks at Igby's one night. Hicks was a brash, brilliant comic, who died of cancer at his parents' home in Arkansas a few years later. He was a favorite of people in the business, but he was, like anchovies, an acquired taste. The night I worked with him, a Sunday, he wandered on stage in a t-shirt and jeans, said he had just come from a wedding in Venice, and added, "You know what's so beautiful about children? Nothing. Fuck children! No, let's make this more personal (pointing at the audience): fuck *your* children!" I had neither the confidence, anger, nor presence to get away with doing the same kind of material. On the other hand, I wasn't sure the 18 or so people in the crowd wanted to hear some guy in a t-shirt telling them how he'd like to fuck their children, even rhetorically.

I also auditioned for a few television shows that year but nothing came of it. I tried to get an agent, but never found one who could help me get any more work than I was already getting. At one of these auditions I met a comic who told me she read somewhere that if you concentrate on doing what you love to do, you'll be rich beyond your dreams. "Great," she said, "so by this time next year, I should have half a million dollars in the bank all by masturbating and going to lunch with my friends."

I found myself leaving L.A. more and more for work on the road, figuring it was more productive than sitting at The Improv bar drinking Calistoga Springs with other comics.

One of these trips took me to Bermuda where I was asked to help book a comedy club. It could have been a great job, but Bermudan customs nixed the deal at the end. I sat in a Holiday Inn in Raleigh Durham for three days trying to get clearance into the country. When I was there, though, my sponsors introduced me to a girl they said was the most beautiful woman on the Island. She very well could have been.

Maggie had short, blonde hair, wire-rimmed glasses, and looked very much like Bridget Fonda, on whom I had an inordinate crush at the time. I don't know why she asked me to dinner, but I remember sitting with her at a seafood restaurant on the banks of the Atlantic Ocean. Up the hill from the restaurant, fireworks were being set off by a big pink hotel, the ocean was literally beneath our feet, and I was having dinner with, for me anyway, Henry Fonda's granddaughter.

"Barry," Maggie asked in a voice part Bermudan, part English, "are you having a good time?"

Looking at the ocean, the fireworks, scallops as big as hamburgers, the sun setting, and a girl whose last name I didn't know, I said, "Let's put it this way: If we wind up in bed tonight it'll be the best night of my life. Even if we don't, it's coming in at number six. This is still better than most of the sex I've ever had."

It was probably the best line I ever delivered to a girl.

We did. And her five orgasms made it into my act—even if she left in tears right after. That, too, made it into the act.

*Is it possible for a woman to have five orgasms . . . and not have a good time?* (Usually agreement from women in the crowd.) *Good. So I'm with this woman a few months ago, and she has five orgasms in forty-five minutes* (pause). *And I'm taking credit. I don't care what you say. Anyway, she has the five, but then leaves. Leaves! I said, "Where you going?" She said, "It's no big deal." "No big deal," I ask. She just had five orgasms, and after giving her five, should she worship at the shrine of Barry? I mean* (pointing to a female in the audience), *if you gave me five, I'm not leaving, I'm Moto the House Boy."*

Months later, when Maggie and I were no longer getting along, I made the mistake of inviting her on a cruise I was working to Ensanada, Mexico. One night on the ship, she heard me do that bit in the show, and said, "By the way, Barry, it was four—*not* five!"

Before the cruise, she called and said she didn't want to have sex anymore, but still wanted to go. I made the mistake of thinking that wouldn't matter. The cabins on these cruises are so small, it's tough enough getting along with each other when you are fucking; when you're not, it's impossible. I thought I'd handle it more maturely, but by the second night, after we spent hours playing a game where I'd push the bunks together and she'd push them apart, I said to her, "Do you realize that there are six billion people in the world. For argument's sake, let's say one percent of those people are on vacation right now: that means roughly sixty million people are in hotels, cruises, ski cabins, whatever. Let's say half of that group, or 30 million people, is getting along. We're not in that group. There are probably 1500 couples on this cruise right now who are or will be having sex very soon. We're not even close to being in that group. In fact, we may be the most miserable couple on vacation in the world right now.

I don't remember what she said, but I do remember the beds being on opposite sides of the cabin.

I blame it in part on being in the wrong ocean. The cruise was through the Pacific; the Atlantic seems older and wiser with more character. It reminded me of that scene in *Atlantic City* when the kid, after seeing the Atlantic Ocean for the first time, mentions to the Burt Lancaster character how beautiful he finds it.

"That's nothing," says Lancaster. "You should have seen it in the old days."

Nobody says that about the Pacific.

What struck me odd about all this was that when I went to Bermuda, the nicest place I had ever been, I went to perform and book a comedy club—not to come away with stories about seafood and fireworks and oceans and sex.

I didn't go into comedy for the women, but many of my stories in one way or another revolve around them. I guess it was the adventure. Even the lost year in North Hollywood, when I remember spending most of it in a sloped loft with leg cramps, I met women who belonged in Robert Altman films.

I met a girl in Redondo Beach who would only have sex with me in her laundry room because she was married and didn't want to be unfaithful in the bed she shared with her husband.

I met another girl who produced sex infomercials and drove a Ferrari (it didn't last because I insisted on taking the Mazda all the time).

I met a girl in Fresno who was convinced her cat knew the actual days of the week and who said to me in bed one morning, "We can keep having sex, but there's no reason to have a relationship. We have nothing in common." I agreed immediately.

I met another girl, who once worked on *The Tonight Show*, and, who, in a park over pizza, said something about the two of us being geographically undesirable and emotionally unavailable, and then added, "I just don't know if what's right for Kitty is right for Barry." "Do we know these people?" I asked.

I met Francesca, one girl to whom I still talk (except maybe after she reads this), a teacher from West Covina, who blacked out one night after oral sex. When she came to, she said, "I thought the first orgasm was good, but oh, man, that second one. What was that thing with the flip?" It would be a running joke for the next six years. In fact, I ran into her roommate years later at The Maxim in Vegas and she asked, "Barry, why don't you tell *me* about that second one?" Francesca also had a vibrator she called *Picasso* and a dildo which remained nameless. She liked bondage, spanking, phone and cybersex, wore benoir balls while teaching her third grade class, but wouldn't have intercourse because she was a Christian and wanted to save that act for her husband. (You can't help but admire such a liberal reading of the Bible.)

It's all pretty embarrassing now—the energy I wasted, even though while it was happening, it didn't seem like I was working that hard. I knew I was wasting a good chunk of my life in comedy, but I kept telling myself that making people laugh, going to matinees, sleeping late, and having sex with a woman on a boat around the "It's a Small World" exhibit at Disneyland is better than being a claims administrator for Equifax. As my friend Marie told me years later, "Barry, you just never let a moment go by, do you?"

Mostly, I missed the kids. I called them three, four times a week and we made plans to take trips together when we could. I elevated my stress-filled leg as much as possible and spent too many evenings leaning against the rail, looking down at the living room. I once heard my roommate's houseguest having phone sex on the brown sofa downstairs. I thought it somehow appropriate, here in L.A., that she was faking an orgasm on a fake leather sofa.

Sitting in the loft one September Saturday, trying to watch television and being convinced that the blood clot would soon dislodge and head for my brain or aorta, I realized I would never be on the cover of *Newsweek* as "the comic voice of the '90s", that I would never host my own late night talk show, that I was a road comic in L.A. with children in Oklahoma who had an insurance man named Bob as a step-father, and that, more to the point, I was miserable. I might regret leaving; I would definitely regret staying. I didn't want the kids forgetting me. I wanted a television that got all the stations, a place to put my clothes, and, most important, I wanted a wall.

It wasn't a difficult decision moving back to Tulsa, so 13 months after I arrived, I banged my head on the ceiling for the last time, and then took the same roads through the same parts of Arizona, New Mexico, Texas, and headed back to Oklahoma. Everything I had still fit into the Mazda.

A year to the day, the Northridge earthquake gutted the condo. Something tells me the iron railing survived.

One more thing: I never did get to see the Grand Canyon. But my leg got better.

## CHAPTER 6

## Olivia's changing breasts

**W**hen I returned to Tulsa from North Hollywood, I was 36. First thing I did was rent an apartment with walls and doors; second thing I did was bring the kids over; unfortunately, they had already been there ... sort of. Unbeknownst to me, I rented an apartment in the same complex in which Bob lived when he met Jane; consequently, the kids knew their way around.

"Hey, Dad, you know they have two pools here and one's indoors. Bob used to ... oh, sorry," Nina told me, as we drove up to the place for the first time. It was almost enough to make me move.

My one-bedroom apartment was 810 square feet with a living and dining room, kitchen, bedroom, a washer and dryer, and a sunroom where the kids would sleep—and not a loft or iron rail in sight. According to the rental agent, I wasn't just getting an apartment for my money, but an entire *lifestyle community*. I asked her if an apartment without the lifestyle was cheaper. I bought a black leather sofa and matching love seat with ottoman, a glass table with an iron pewter bottom, and four black folding chairs because, apparently, that's how divorced 36-year-old men furnish their apartments. Jane gave me some of our old red dishes, now chipped, a few mismatched glasses, and our bedroom chest of drawers.

Somewhere, I came across a 12-inch black and white television, which I put near the fireplace. I almost burned down the apartment one Super Bowl Sunday, and probably would have had Paul not asked, "Hey, Dad, is the side of the television supposed to be melting like this?" Disfigured and lopsided, but still on the fireplace, it still got more stations than the TV in North Hollywood—even if they were in black and white and you had to sit three feet away to see them.

#!!°?)*%#*!( • ?#

Since I had never lived alone in a real apartment, I needed everything. I bought wash cloths, which I never used, enough ketchup, mustard, and mayonnaise to gain me acceptance in the Mormon church, a 12-pack of Comet, 24 kitchen sponges, 9 dish rags, a cutting board, a cheap set of knives, and then I went to Walmart and bought an even cheaper set of generic Teflon pots and pans, which started chipping as soon as I took them out of the box. I also bought baking soda, which I put in back of the refrigerator, but never opened.

A guy named Grover, who made beds on the bad side of Tulsa, made me a California King, and then I went to Target and bought sheets nearly as ugly as what I had in Joan's loft. God knows why, but I also bought a mattress cover; something a grown man should never buy alone. I drew the line at pillow shams and bed skirts. I bought a doormat, which read *What the hell are you doing here?* (Years later, when it came time to pick out an e-mail address, I chose *Vuzvilla*, which is Yiddish for *What do you want?*) I then went to Bed, Bath and Beyond and got a big pink candle. I had a black candleholder and I thought the two would look good together. They didn't, but the candle came in handy a few years later when a girl from Texas chose to masturbate with it while lying on my clichéd sofa. It seemed wrong to put the candle in anything else after that.

Grover also made a trundle bed for Nina and Paul, which filled up the sunroom, but it mostly went unused, as they still liked sleeping with me.

The kids and I had themes for the days they came over. Mondays were "Mall Night," where we'd go to Sears and play on the riding lawnmowers until a clerk would tell us to stop; Tuesdays were "Monster Meatball Night," where I'd make them spaghetti with meatballs the size of small cantaloupes; Wednesdays were "Bagel Days," where we'd wake up early and, before I took them to school, eat bagels and cream cheese and drink fountain Coke for breakfast; Thursdays were "Candy Day" at Mr. Bulky's, where we each got a half-pound limit on any candy; Fridays were "Pizza Night" at Mario's Pizza, where the kids would make *suicides* and play with pizza dough before the meals arrived; Saturdays were "Video Arcade Day," as long as one of us could find a 2-for-1 token coupon; and Sundays were "Movie Day," where we'd go to a dollar movie and smuggle in our own popcorn and beverages. At night, I continued to tell them stories. Once I told Nina a story about a mom, a dad, and the birth of a baby in a great big pink hospital, but didn't say it was the story of *her* birth. "That's me, isn't it?" she said after hearing about the daddy who told jokes for a living. "You know Dad, you and mom could get back together if you just said 'sorry' to each other."

The Mazda, which the kids renamed the *Comedy Car*, passed 100,000 miles. They took turns sitting up front and willingly paid the dime fines I assessed whenever they forgot to wear seatbelts. As much as anything, I liked being their dad—even if I could only give them an alcove for a bedroom and big hamburgers from a peeling Teflon pan. Once, I took them to Bell's, an amusement park in Tulsa, and Paul met a girl while waiting in line at the roller coaster. They hung out with each other most of the day while Nina and I played skeet ball and collected prize tickets.

"Maybe we should have stayed?" Paul asked on the drive home. "I mean, I really liked this girl. What if I never see her again? You think I should have?"

"There are people who'll tell you that you only get three chances at love. You're 11 now, which means if she was one of your three, and you live to 90, then you've got 79 years to go and you've only got two left."

"Shit!" he said.

"No, it's okay. She probably isn't one of your three, but next time you have a feeling like that, don't talk yourself out of it. You stay at the roller coaster as long as you need to. Fate's a wonderful thing, Paul, but some-times you need a phone number and an address for it to do any good. And one more thing: don't say *shit* in front of your father. What the hell's wrong with you?"

The next day Paul called me.

"You never guess who goes to my school? The girl from *Bell's*! She eats lunch the same time I do. Can you believe it? I didn't even know she was in my school and now I find out that we have the same lunch peri-od. Hey, Dad, I got my three back."

Two days later Jane called me.

"What is this about you telling Paul he only gets three chances at love?"

"Well, I want him to know that sometimes love hits you at strange times, and that you may only get four-and-a-half seconds or so to do something about it—especially if you're leaving the roller coaster and she's staying."

"I don't know why you're telling an eleven-year-old that. Anyway, was I one for you?" she asked.

"One what?"

"One of your three."

"Oh, please . . ."

". . . No, was I?"

"I don't know. Ask Bob if you're one of his three."

"You mean to tell me after giving you two kids, I didn't even make your Top Three list?"

"All right, if it's that important, you're one of my three."

*Fuck*, I thought, *I'm out*. I always believed I had one left.

And this was one of our milder conversations.

Before I came back to Tulsa, I wondered if I'd have any regret leav-ing Los Angeles. I not only didn't, but the only time I even thought about leaving was when I thought about how much I never thought about it. I still wondered if my career would ever amount to anything, but at least I did so while driving Paul and Nina to the arcade. I still found myself staring at the ceiling at odd hours, still had trouble sleeping through the night, still fought with Jane (she was under the impression that my new interest in fatherhood was just an act), but it was better going through it in Tulsa. I had four walls. And, apparently, a lifestyle.

Work was steady. By the mid '90s, I was working in Vegas at the Maxim Hotel 12 weeks a year, while doing the Riviera two or three weeks as well. I was doing Catch a Rising Star in Princeton and Philadelphia, the Atlantis in the Bahamas, Don's club in Houston, the Laff Stop in Austin and a few others. I even played a club in Albuquerque with a feature act who stabbed the opening act with a fork. We were all at dinner when the opener, who was annoying the feature all week anyway, kept picking French fries off the guy's plate. The feature told him to stop; he didn't. So the next time the opener reached for a fry, the feature stabbed him in the back of his hand with a fork.

"I told you to leave my fucking fries alone."

The opener looked at me as if to confirm that there was, indeed, a fork in the back of his hand.

"The only thing I can say," I said, "is I wouldn't touch his burger."

It was schizophrenic at times. Snuggling with my kids one night; watching comics knife each other over fries the next. And then, of course, there were the women I met on the road. In Evansville, after a show, a waitress met me in the parking lot and told me she was a lesbian in a committed relationship, but was curious about what it would be like to sleep with a man.

"Are you asking me or are you *asking* me?" I said.

"I don't know myself," she said.

In the morning as I walked her out of the apartment the club provided for comedians, we saw the other comic in his bathrobe, sitting on the sofa, watching the Clarence Thomas-Anita Hill hearings on television.

"She's not great, but I'd fuck her," he conceded, pointing to Hill.

Any wonder some women are in committed lesbian relationships.

Which brings me to Olivia, who was my age, 36, when I met her, but looked ten years younger than I did. Her breasts at the time we met—and this is important—were small and perky, which fit nicely with the rest of her 5'3" frame. In the year that followed, though, she would have them enlarged for one guy, whom she would marry and divorce within seven months and for whom she would also legally change her first name. She would also marry again, get pregnant, dye her hair black, emaciate herself, and be diagnosed with bi-polar disorder, but I don't want you to pre-judge. She has eyes the color of Halls Ice Blue Mentho-Lyptus Drops, a disarming smile, and when the stars were aligned right, an agile, complex mind. When they weren't in line, her mind was more like clam chowder. She lived in Austin, but I first met her on a TWA flight to St. Louis. She was with her daughter; I was with an early copy of my divorce decree.

I called her a few times after that plane trip, and then, when I worked the Laff Stop in Austin again, I invited her to the show. When I saw her, she still had the clear blue eyes and the smile, but she looked like she had four breasts—two stacked on either side. I had never seen such big tits on such a small girl.

"You like?" she asked as I met her at the restaurant before the show.

"What's not to like?"

"Yeah, well, they're not supposed to be this big. I was supposed to get C cups, but the doctor read the chart wrong or I checked the wrong box. Anyway, he gave me D's instead. I kind of like them, though. What do you think?"

"I think you should sue. Or send a thank-you card."

After the show, we went out to Katz' Deli by the state capital. She told me she had just gotten divorced, had just started working at Dell Computer as a programmer, and then asked why I wasn't headlining.

"I don't know. Maybe it's as simple as the other guy being funnier."

"But he's not, that's what bothers me. You're funnier than he is, but nobody noticed."

"Why?"

God, her tits were huge.

"Because you won't let them. When you're on stage, you give off the impression that the audience is doing *you* the favor by letting you be there; the other comic lets them know they're lucky he showed up. The audience liked you more as a person, but they respected him more as a comedian. I think he's headlining because the club people, or whoever is in charge of such things, thinks he acts more like one. The audience does, too."

I've always been a sucker for girls like Olivia—girls who can unearth truth one minute and then check the wrong cup size on a breast implant form the next. I find the struggle they make just to get through the day, or just where to put the verb, dramatically sexy. Did I endow the moment with too much? Of course. With girls like Olivia, there was always a day or two in the month (maybe just an hour) when they were remarkably sane, giving, and wonderful. Of course the other 28 days they were fucking lunatics, but if you caught them at the right time, they could make it difficult for you to ever love anyone else as much.

Over a 3AM snack of jellybeans and Sprite, she told me she enlarged her breasts for a guy she had been dating. There were complications during the surgery, however, so she was bedridden for seven weeks immediately afterwards. The guy never came over to check on her, never called, and started dating someone else during her recuperation.

"So you're telling me you got your breasts enlarged for a guy who never saw them, touched them, or kissed them?"

"Pretty crazy, huh?"

Not compared to what followed.

After I left Austin, she called six or seven times a day for the next two months, and when I'd answer, she'd say *Hello* with more intensity, passion, and seduction than was really necessary. She'd come on the road with me; I'd spend weekends with her in Austin. She just about had me convinced no woman would ever love me as much when she called me in Charlotte, North Carolina to tell me she was marrying her gym trainer. "Barry Friedman, Hi. It's Olivia."

Two things. First: whenever a girl calls me by my full name, I know I'm in trouble; second, without that *Hello* of hers, Olivia was almost unrecognizable.

She told me she was working on weights one day when she met a man who was very much like me.

"But, Barry, you I can't have. Him, I can."

Before she hung up, she told me she would someday see me in heaven. Not *have a nice life* or *it was great meeting you* or even *I loved our time together*, but *I'll see you in heaven.*

I was angry, sad, confused, and frustrated—everything but surprised.

An hour later, while watching MTV, I heard the Eric Clapton song she stole the "heaven" line from.

The following year, I was scheduled to work Austin again, and I kept debating in the weeks leading up to the date whether I'd call her. I arrived at the hotel on a Tuesday afternoon, around two o'clock; at 2:30, I called. I got her answering machine.

*Hi, if this message is for Olivia or Beth, leave your message now.*

I called back.

"Olivia, hi, it's Barry. How are you? And who's Beth? Did you get a roommate?"

"No, it's me."

"No, it's not you," I laughed. "You're Olivia. Who's Beth?"

"Barry, I *am* Beth. I mean I'm both."

"Okay, now I'm lost."

"I mean I'm both. I changed my first name."

This, apparently, was one of the other 28 days.

"What do you mean, you changed your *first* name? Why?"

"Barry, listen, remember when I got married?"

"Yeah."

"Well, my husband..."

"The guy you knew for ten days that you met at the gym?"

"Fuck you! But, yes, the guy I met at the gym hated the name Olivia. He said it sounded like an old woman, so as a wedding gift, I changed my name to Beth."

"Most guys would have settled for a watch. I mean, you're joking, right? You didn't really change your first name, did you?"

"Yeah, I did."

"How do you do that? Do you tell the judge that your parents fucked up when they named you Olivia?"

"Pretty much. They really don't ask for an explanation."

"That's convenient, huh?"

"You think this is all pretty weird?"

"The breast enlargement, no; the marriage after ten days, no. The name change, well, I gotta tell you, you lose me a little."

"I know, I know. And I could tell you I never loved him, that I was just getting over you, and that he helped me, but what's the point? He *did* remind me of you, though, Barry, but..."

"...I never would have asked you to change your name. And what do you mean 'getting over me'? Who told you that you had to get over me?"

"The point is, Barry, we got divorced and I'm living alone with my daughter. He was a little abusive, too."

Of course, I invited her to dinner and the show. (I'm a high school drama queen sometimes.) When I saw Olivia, she had the look of a woman on the right medication but the wrong dosage. She was alternately hyper and lethargic. Her breasts were normal-size again, but her hair was cut embarrassingly close to her scalp. She was thin enough to have come from Auschwitz.

"What happened to those?" I asked, pointing at her breasts.

"Well, my husband didn't like them big, so I had them reduced."

"You changed your name *and* reduced your breasts for this guy?"

"Am I going to wind up in your act?"

"Count on it. You know, Olivia, Beth—can we pick one?—maybe you should stop fucking around with the size of your breasts. What if the next guy just wants you to have one—right in the middle of your chest? What are you going to do then?"

She came to the show; I still wasn't headlining.

As we leaned against the car in the Austin Laff Stop parking lot after the show, she told me about her bi-polar disorder.

"It's like there are two of me inside me and they don't like each other."

I didn't know what to say, so I kissed her. I just hope I kissed the right one.

She called a few months later to say she had dyed her hair black, had quit her job, had met a guy, was moving to Houston, was getting married, and, oh yeah, was pregnant.

The following year, when I worked the Houston Laff Stop, I wanted to call, but was afraid I might get the other one.

I never heard from her again, but Don called me during the FBI raid in Waco to say he thought he had seen Olivia running around the compound ... *trying to get back in.*

He was joking ... I think.

CHAPTER 7

# Just one big infomercial for Barry

here's a story, based on some truth, about a comedian who loses to a mime on Star Search. You need to know what comics think of mimes to know how humiliating this is. Everywhere the comic goes, he hears things like, "How could you lose to a clown?" and "Hey, maybe if you had worn a red nose, things might have turned out differently." Soon, the guy is so angry about this—blaming the show itself for favoring acts with bright, shiny objects over monologists with a point of view—that he begins to trash the mime's reputation to club managers, agents, and other performers. He then feels guilty, so, being a good Catholic, goes to his priest to ask for forgiveness for his pettiness and jealousy. He receives absolution, but as he's leaving the confessional, the priest says, "Pssst, did you really lose to a fucking mime?"

Comics who do straight stand-up have little use for those who don't.

As for magicians, I could never understand their appeal. The dollar bill is obviously not in the lemon when they cut into it, the girl is not really in the box that's being sawed in half, and they can't all hate Copperfield as much as they say they do. There's a story that Jay Leno once stopped in to the Comedy and Magic Club in Hermosa Beach to do a set just as a magician was coming off stage. As Leno stepped over used firecrackers, streamers, bags, toys, and Jell-O, he looked down and called to the magician backstage, "Hey, d'you *write* all this?"

Ventriloquists, to me, are not comics; they're carpenters. They build their comedy, literally, from wood. And their acts are all based on the premise that the dummy just can't be controlled. Watch one. Count how many times the ventriloquist admonishes his dummy to stick to the script, do the joke, and act appropriately. *I can't believe it, folks. This has never happened before.* Finally, so frustrated, the ventriloquist will put his "partner" back in the trunk (where it will still get off a few more good lines) and then the ventriloquist will once again apologize profusely. He'll then offer to give his buddy one more chance to do the show as written, and then, returning from the trunk, the dummy will of course do anything but. Sometimes, the relationship between the ventriloquist and his sidekick is one for Freud. I've seen guys stroke their dummy's hair, pick out its clothes with the diligence of a new parent, and argue with it over the previous night's show.

The best one I ever saw was Willie Tyler. Aside from being technically proficient (some ventriloquists look like they're dubbing a Japanese war movie into English), Willie treated his puppet Lester like, well, a puppet. As soon as the show was over, Willie would throw Lester in a fucking gym bag and toss it in the dressing room until the next show. When people would ask Willie where Lester was, he'd say, "Lester doesn't do interviews."

As for guitar acts, they're impossible to follow on stage. No matter how high-energy, no matter how brilliant, a monologist can never excite the crowd the way the first eight bars of *Sweet Home Alabama* can.

I heard of a comedian who worked with a bird. At the end of the guy's act, his pigeon would fly out of the cage and then return on command. Once in the middle of a hot July night, the bird flew out and got caught in one of the ceiling fans and died an ugly and messy death. There was bird shit and feathers on tables and in people's drinks and hair. The comic was so distraught, he couldn't continue the show, and walked off stage. Later that night, as a waitress was cleaning up bird remains, she said to the other comic working the week, "You know, I don't know how much birds cost, but if he could kill a bird every night, these crowds would love it."

To many of these novelty acts, there was nothing particularly brilliant about what monologists did either. To them, we were all just bitching about girlfriends and cops and the ingredients in Chicken McNuggets. And other than a few pointed remarks about Jane marrying a bald insurance agent and flirting with Anson Williams, "Potsie" of *Happy Days*, I didn't have much in my act that distinguished me from what the other 463,000 Jewish monologists from Long Island had in theirs. On stage, I didn't juggle fluorescent green balls, fart the first few bars of "Born to be Wild," or caress inflatable dolls. I simply talked. The problem with doing that is that I had no hook. Unlike the ventriloquist, who can have a cross-dressing midget puppet, or a magician, who can make toupees disappear, or even a hypnotist, who can make you think you're naked at an outdoor barbecue, I had to keep people's attention with whatever passed for my wit. A monologist can rely on his personality or looks, but that's tricky. A girl in Vegas told me I looked like one of the Baldwin brothers, but she didn't say which one. With my luck, the Baldwins have a brother named Manny, who's an accountant with thinning hair, and that's who the girl had in mind.

I worked with the microphone in its stand, and I stood behind it, figuring it was easier for the crowd to focus on a stationary target than a moving one. Carrot Top, who does have a trunk of props (and a trunk full of money as well) told me once, "You guys [monologists] can talk about that stuff; I can't." He even has a bit in his act that goes something like, "If I ever said on stage 'I was with my girlfriend last night,' you (the audience) would look at me and say 'no you weren't.'"

I, however, could, so I did. I also talked about Billy Joel's eyes having the appearance of a thyroid condition; under-worked prostitutes in Vegas who should consider running a sale every once in awhile; talking bathroom scales that tell the offending party to *get off*; my dad's toupee and the ability of even Ray Charles to know it doesn't look good; Christian outlet malls where the "Christ is coming in 2000" shirts are on clearance; and the contradiction of having separate toothbrushes after engaging in oral sex. It is known as observational comedy. I usually wore a suit on stage, figuring most of the audience worked harder that day than I would in a week so they'd appreciate the fact that I showered and changed clothes. Audiences, especially the men, look at comics with a combination of admiration and disgust: and not just because we're trying to get their girlfriends in bed. Comedians get paid for doing something most people know how to do.

Comedians, however, tell jokes to people we don't know for upwards of an hour. Making your friends laugh at an oyster bar for a few minutes during Happy Hour is easier than doing so to 14 bored New Yorkers at a club in Greenwich Village at two in the morning. For me, I had an ex-wife who married an insurance agent a month after my divorce; I had a peculiar affinity for women who had more breast scars, first names, and husbands than is probably healthy; and I was one of about 17 Jews living in Oklahoma. One of the difficulties in comedy is making your perspective universal enough for people to enjoy. There are more than 17 Jews in Oklahoma, obviously (really, there are), but making an audience believe, as I tried to do, that wearing a Yarmulke makes most in Tulsa think I'm stealing a salad plate is a different challenge than making your co-workers laugh with a joke about two lesbians talking to St. Peter.

There are more important things to do with your life than to tell jokes about ex-wives and psycho girlfriends; on the other hand, how do you turn down $1750 for three shows on a cruise from Tampa to the Cayman Islands? Bill Cosby said it takes a comedian ten years to find out who he is on stage. On my tenth anniversary, I was in Las Vegas at the Maxim, opening for a guy with a lisp.

The epiphany didn't happen.

Good comedy isn't always truth, but it's usually nearby. Further, even though most comedy is performed alone, it's a dialogue, and like any conversation, much of what's going on is unspoken. I knew an open-miker, a born-again Christian (usually a bad combination), who had a sweet, unassuming personality on stage.

He did a joke in which he cautioned the audience to not rely too heavily on the accuracy of the maps in the back of the bible. They tend to change, he said, without much warning.

The audience wasn't buying it.

By contrast, the late Sam Kinison, with whom I worked a few times, told a joke about Jim Baker when he, Baker, was relased from prison the first time. It seems Baker had gone back to television evangelism and—this surprised Kinison—was successfully raising money again.

"What does this guy have to do," asked Kinison, "before people start believing he's a fraud? Take his cock out and jerk off on the screen?"

The audience roared.

How to explain why an insightful joke about religion died and one about semen splattering on a TV screen worked is one of the beautiful mysteries of comedy. How to explain why some comics are considered geniuses instead of fat guys in berets saying *fuck* a lot is another.

A woman in Houston came up to me after a show at Don's club and said, "You are the best looking Jewish man I have ever seen."

When I asked her to explain, she said, "Don't get me wrong, you're a good-looking guy, but for a Jewish guy, you're outstanding."

"What did you say?"

"Why? Isn't that a compliment? You *are* a good-looking Jew."

"Forget it," I said. "What about the act?"

"Who cares? You're gorgeous. More people are looking at you than listening. That's your strength. Other comics have to work harder than you."

A few weeks later at The Comedy Zone in Charlotte, I closed my show with a new bit. I asked a married man in the audience if he had ever thought about infidelity. When he said no, I did the following:

*What if there's no hell, no heaven, no God? Or what if there is a God but when you get there, you find out he's not that strict. That's got to piss you off. Can you imagine? You spend your whole life being faith-*

*ful, and you get up there and some guy meets you and says, "Remember that girl in Charlotte? You should have fucked her."*

Later, the headliner, Etta May, and I were standing in the karaoke pit in the lounge outside the club. I had just finished singing Dylan's "Knocking on Heaven's Door" when May came over and joined me at a table.

"How do you get away with that?"

"What?"

"Doing a joke about God giving you permission to fuck around?"

"I don't follow you."

"I'm thinking your strength on stage is not your writing; it's you. Maybe you get away with it because they like you."

"Funny you should mention that," I said. "A woman in Houston pretty much told me the same thing."

"It's true," May said excitedly.

"It is not."

"Look, it doesn't matter what you say, your strength is that, you can talk about what you do: fantasies, infidelities, whatever—and you'll get away with it because people like you. They like looking at you."

"That blows."

"Oh you're a good, clever writer, apparently sensitive, but look at what you talk about. You bring up the fact that you gave a woman five orgasms in an hour, you tell us about your kids, you show us you're intelligent. Essentially, what you're saying is, "Aren't I cute? Don't you want to sleep with me?"

"I do *not* do that!"

"Oh, come on, Barry, if you could, you'd bring a full-length mirror on stage with you."

"Can you do that?"

Etta laughed. I laughed.

"It's just one big infomercial for Barry, isn't it?"

CHAPTER 8

## Sun screen

n the Bahamas, it seems, if you have a car and a stencil set, you can be in the taxi business. Cabs have meters that are never used, windows that are often stuck, and shocks that need replacement. There are enough stray dogs on this island to film a Steven King novel, a half gallon of orange juice can cost seven dollars, gratuities are added to everything, including take-out, and losing your heart is as easy as losing your luggage.

I've lost both here and never got either back. But the Bahamas are also great for second chances.

On the beaches, large native women with t-shirts, trinkets, and jewelry over one arm, plod across the sand, looking to braid the hair of American college students on spring break, vacationing Germans, and visiting Asians who can't speak English. Young, scary, well-built Bahamian men hawk Jet Ski, parasailing, and booze cruise trips while hotel security guards try to evict them for trespassing. At night, both will be at Club Waterloo, The Zoo, and Rock N Roll groping college girls from places like East Lansing and Storrs. Richard Bethel, the club owner and my best friend down here, says that *Jungle Fever* sets in for many of these girls.

"They wouldn't even talk to these guys back home, but down here, they'd fuck one of them on a lifeguard chair at three in the morning. It makes it tough for the rest of us."

Not that Richard is at all like the rest of us. He weighs 315 pounds, rarely wears socks, and looks like a Columbian drug lord; with his ponytail, great skin, and engaging smile. He drives around the island in a maroon Cadillac while drinking Meyers rum and Coke and half a lime from a 44 ounce Big Gulp cup. His mother was Canadian; his father was a black Bahamian, which explains both his citizenship and his accent. And, oh yeah, he married his father's mistress.

The first time I came down to work at Joker's Wild was a month before my divorce. I asked Jane to join me, but she thought it was a transparent attempt to get her to reconsider dumping me, which, of course, it was.

"You're such a con artist, Barry."

"Yeah, maybe so, but even con artists have feelings," I said, which is exactly what a con artist would say.

My first trip, in the summer of 1992, was without her. We divorced on schedule.

I don't snorkel, scuba dive, or jet ski. Nor do I pet the dolphins, swim with the sharks, para-sail, or even like sitting in the sun that much. In short, I don't like to do anything that makes this place popular; still, I love being here. A girlfriend of mine, who sounded much like Edie Falco on *The Sopranos*, wondered if that had to do with my being away from the ambivalence and obstacles in my life that got in the way of comedy. In the Bahamas, there were no children to remind me how much of their lives I was missing, no ex-wife reminding me how much and how often I ruined her life; moreover, there were no friends with better jobs, nor bemused parents, siblings with rivalries, or apartments without proper furnishings. She was right; we, the comedy and I, got along better down here than anywhere else. Besides, I liked the ocean being as close as it was.

In the early '90s, there were only a few flights a day into what passes for Paradise International Airport; the vast majority flew into Nassau International. (They all do now, as the airport in Paradise is being bulldozed to build condos.)

When the kids were small, though, there was still service from Miami and Fort Lauderdale to Paradise on the kind of planes that usually crash into Iowa cornfields. Nina, who was tired from the trip, started throwing a fit in the room that night. She threw herself on the floor, and when I told her if she didn't start behaving, I was going to send her home, she immediately stopped, looked up at me, stopped crying, and said with perfect timing, "Like where are you going to get a plane?"

*They lost my luggage at the airport and, of course, being in the Bahamas, they got right on that problem.*

There's a rhythm down here, somewhere between laid-back and comatose. It's maddening at first, but quickly becomes infectious.

Joker's Wild is at the Atlantis Hotel. The club was here when Merv Griffin owned the place, here when Donald Trump owned the place. It used to be that you couldn't make fun of the maid or waitress service, the casino odds, or, since he owned it, Merv Griffin (or his weight) but since he sold it to Sol Kirzner, of Sun City, the rules changed. Merv took quite a beating after that. The club moves every year or so within the casino, usually because the hotel brass decides the space can be better used for a row of slot machines or a buffet. The club always manages to survive, though. For a few years in the early '90s, Joker's Wild had another venue at Crystal Palace, a hotel on Cable Beach in Nassau, and that's where I first worked. Since then, all my dates have been at the hotel on Paradise Island.

The gig here lasts two weeks, is only six nights a week, and there's only one show a night. In a year, then, there are only 52 comics who get to work it (26 headliners, 26 features); consequently, it's in demand. Creative Entertainment out of Charlotte, North Carolina, and its president, Brad Greenberg, booked Joker's Wild for years. Most of Creative's gigs were strings of one-nighters throughout the southeast, but they did have weeklong rooms in Jacksonville, Memphis, Charlotte, and Orlando, all of which paid less than the one-nighters, but, obviously, entailed much less travel. Brad also had a room in the Cayman Islands for a few years, which I played a half dozen times.

Brad's claim to fame was that he managed Carrot Top for a number of years. I heard Carrot was selling shoes when he started going to Open Mike Nights at the Comedy Zone in Charlotte when Brad discovered him. There are millions of stories about Brad and his business practices and acumen, but none better than the one about his booking a wrestling bear for a time. When Greenberg was first starting out managing acts, he had a bear that he used to book in clubs. Men would challenge the bear in the ring. This made Brad (and apparently the bear) a lot of money. Mike West, a southern comic I started out with, used to do a lot of work for Brad. When he heard about the wrestling bear, he told me, "My goal, Shecky (that was his nickname for me), is to make more money than that fucking bear."

I met more girls in the Bahamas than anywhere else, with the exception of Vegas. I met Claudia, but she gets her own chapter; a cabin girl named, I swear, Inga; a Japanese tour guide, who didn't understand a word of English, but loved watching American comedians; a girl from New Hampshire with a tulip bulb tattoo around her navel; an English girl the day Princess Diana died, who said she wouldn't fuck me because she had just fucked another guy 16 hours earlier and didn't, as she said, want me to think that all she does "is fuck"; a married woman, about to get divorced, who bought me a $400 watch with money her soon-to-be ex-husband gave her from his gambling winnings; a Canadian prostitute, who said there would be no "ka ching" outside of her own country; and a Maryland high school sophomore, who swore to me that sex with a 16-year old in the Bahamas was legal. I passed on that one.

Another time, a few weeks after my divorce, I met a 21-year-old girl, and her mom, who was 43. I was 35 at the time. The next day, the girl and I were sitting at the pool when she told me that her mother had a crush on me. I was flattered, but thought, what would I want with the mother when I can have the daughter? Then I realized her mother was younger than Jane. The daughter asked me about the youngest girl I ever slept with and then said she had done everything sexually a girl could do.

"Well," she said, "I mean, I haven't had anal sex or been with another woman or even been tied up."

"Then in my book, you're not even close to having done everything. What *have* you done?" I asked.

"Well, one time, I made love on the floor."

"Scandalous. You know, if all works out, you may have a few more stories to tell by the time you leave."

I did tell her the next morning that I was not going to tell anyone about the necktie or the spanking or the light bondage, and I wouldn't be bringing it up now, if she hadn't said, "Hey, tell anyone you want, because if you don't think I'm going to tell my sorority sisters about what you did to me, you're out of your fucking mind."

*After sex, a man wants to sleep, a woman wants to talk. Personally, I want to be untied.*

A note here about the bondage: I tied her hands lightly—and I mean lightly—to the latticework of the headboard with a necktie that had roosters on it. She could have gotten out at any time. I didn't even know how to make a real knot; as such, I tied her hands in a bow. I guess she must have liked it, because, the next morning, as I was kissing her stomach, I felt this tap on the back of my head. When I looked up, I saw these big brown University of Florida freshman sorority-pledged eyes. What she said next was possibly the sexiest thing I ever heard from a woman.

"Go get the tie."

But it wasn't just the sun or the women or the lifeguard chair, where, parenthetically, I discovered the girl from New Hampshire had that tattoo, which made the Bahamas special. It was the comedy. The backdrop helped, but it was the laughs and standing ovations from the crowds through the years at Joker's Wild; it was Richard raising his Bic lighter in the back of the showroom because some woman had just taken off her bra on stage; it was the people who came up to me at the pool to say thanks and tell me a joke; and, ultimately, it was being able to convince myself for at least two weeks every year that I was a success. I had made it as a comedian.

On the other hand, the Bahamas can fool you.

I was once sitting in the pool when four insurance men, who had won a free trip to Atlantis, came and joined me. They had seen the show and wanted to know if I would join them for a drink. I told them no. One of the guys got pretty obnoxious and started gargling beer and telling racist jokes and saying, "You know, I should be on stage. I'm a funny fucker. You don't even know how to party, Barry."

"Look," I said to him, "whether I know how to party or not, I get paid to tell jokes in the Bahamas; you get paid to sell disability from the trunk of your car. I win."

But he probably makes more than the fucking bear.

## CHAPTER 9

# Fear and loafing in Las Vegas

ike many comics starting out, I had to drive to the work. For one thing, I couldn't afford to fly; for another, there was no way to fly. Guymon, Oklahoma, Arnold's Park, Iowa, and Ozark, Alabama do not have airports with connecting service to or from Dodge City, Kansas, Hastings, Nebraska, and Bossier City, Louisiana. Many of them don't even have airports. And that was the thing with doing these one-nighters: the routing would often go from small town to small town and from state to state. A week might start in a place like Fort Walton Beach, Florida on Monday and then go to Ozark, Alabama on Tuesday to Dustin, Florida on Wednesday to Savannah, Georgia on Thursday and then back to Tallahassee, Florida for the weekend.

These gigs were either in hotel lounges or local bars, and comics would usually get paid, in cash, each night after the show, so by the end of the week we might have over 1000 dollars on hand. Those with bills or ex-wives might stop at a 7-11 or an Albertson's and buy a money order and send it to the appropriate place; those who didn't have responsibilities (or those who just didn't own up to them) bought drinks, tipped waitresses too extravagantly, or bought video games and electronic toys. When comedy was booming in the middle and late '80s, there was enough work to keep a comedian on the road 40 to 45 weeks a year.

My friend Mike West, who I told you about, is from Calhoun City, Mississippi, and he worked as a mechanic at Tinker Air Force Base in Midwest City, Oklahoma, and as a cotton picker before doing stand-up. "It was hot, miserable work, and I used to be out there with all these old black men who were singing these old gospel songs while they picked. It was awful because I didn't know the words."

As things began to tighten up, though, a weekday might fall out, leaving the comedian stranded in some cheap hotel in the middle of Louisiana. Doing roadwork is depressing enough when you're working a Howard Johnson lounge in Shreveport, Louisiana; but spending a Wednesday night in a Days Inn in Monroe at your own expense is another level of sadness altogether.

George Campbell, who had the funniest clean act of any comic I ever worked with, told me that he was once doing a string of rooms in northern Florida with a comic, who just happened to be a very tall, 300 pound black woman. As is often the case with these one-nighters, George and the tall black woman took one car in an attempt to share expenses. Now, George is about 5'8," 145 pounds and, this is important to the story, white. Anyway, they stopped at Texaco, and while the attendant was pumping the gas, the guy looked suspiciously at George, and then at the female comic who towered over George, and asked, "Y'all related?"

While I drove to many gigs, I never drove as much as some other comics. For one thing, I never had a car I fully trusted. The Comedy Car, with its temperamental air conditioner, torn driver's seat upholstrey, and squeaky windshield wipers never broke down, but always seemed like it was on the verge. I used to drive past service stations and calculate how far I would have to walk back if the car broke down. As I knew nothing about car maintenance—I once drove 1500 miles with the brake light on—I patted the car a lot and thanked it for never breaking down.

Other comics I knew took work on the road for months on end, crossing the country like drunks trying to walk a straight line. They traveled with VCRs, suitcases filled with clothes and books, coolers, and files full of pictures, tapes, and resumes. Many of them had more in their cars than in their homes.

When I drove, I only took what I needed for the particular week. I never wanted to get comfortable in the car, and thought it was important to feel the humiliation and exhaustion driving from city to city, doing one-nighters in smoky bars, dimly-lit lounges, and redecorated VFW halls. I thought if I made my life easy on the road, I'd never be motivated to leave it. More than hating to drive, I hated spending all that time with myself. On the 8-hour trip from Sioux City, Iowa to Rapid City, South Dakota, I drank 20-ounce Cokes from plastic bottles, ate Big Grab Pretzels and Arby's Beef N Cheddars, listened to Rush Limbaugh and farm reports, metronomically looked at a discounted Rand McNally road map I bought at Wal-Mart, and tried to remember every girl I had slept with since high school. (Years later, on a red-eye flight from Vegas to Houston, I updated the list, writing down their names on an airline sickness bag.)

One weekend in New Orleans, during December of 1990, the coldest weekend of the century in that city, I was picked up at the comedy apartment by the club's assistant manager, who asked me where I was from. After telling him that I was from New York but now lived in Tulsa, I asked him the same question.

"Here," he said.

And in the moment that followed, I had no idea where *here* was. Luckily a *David Duke for President* sign on a telephone pole reminded me where I was. (I heard one comedian say on stage the following night, "Okay, so Louisiana? What is that . . . half French, half swamp-thing?")

I drove to Rapid City, where I saw a sign on the club's entrance *suggesting* patrons leave their firearms in a car. I drove to a club in St. Petersburg, Florida, where the other comic was arrested for having sex with his dog. The comic maintained it was consensual. (This was not the last time I heard of such things. A bartender at the MGM told me he had gone to a party in Vegas once and walked in on a waitress sitting on the edge of a bed, and saw a kitten licking peanut butter off her crotch. The waitress left her job and the city shortly thereafter, proving that even Vegas has some standards.) I drove to a club in Columbus, Mississippi, where the bartender asked me if all Jews were funny.

"I don't know," I said, "are all Baptists stupid?"

On the road, while driving, I spent hours thinking about identity, purpose, fatherhood, my career, and the perfect woman.

I worked more of these venues than I'd ever remember, and I tried to remember them all.

My first real road gig, if you don't count the Omaha gig, was in Sioux Falls, South Dakota. I worked with Dan Bradley, who had seen me perform at an Open Mike Night in Tulsa. He was gracious to offer me the gig (he was headlining and told the club people he wanted me to feature), gracious to pick me up at the airport in Omaha, and gracious to drive me to Sioux Falls. It was in Sioux Falls that I first heard applause that seemed genuine. On the drive home, I asked Dan how the show went and whether I was good enough to do this.

"Fuck, yeah. What'd you think of my set? God, this is great, huh? We're such whores sometimes for needing this much attention."

He was right: about it, about us.

Dan told me that the best you could hope for when you did the road was to work with a comic who wouldn't drain the fucking life out of you. "You're not an asshole," he told me.

Sadly, in late 1999, Dan threw himself off a balcony in a Houston hotel with a sheet tied tightly around his neck.

I never got to tell him that he wasn't an asshole, either.

On the road, there are one-nighters and weeklong rooms. The one-nighters are almost always in or near a hotel. In the weeklong rooms, the club would provide apartments, known as comedy *condos*, for the comedians. These condos were rented, clubs maintained, to give the comedians a sense of home while traveling. In reality, they were rented to save the clubs money on hotel costs. One club in New Mexico even went so far as to put a lock box on the thermostat so the owner could control utility costs.

Instead of hiring a professional cleaning service, managers of clubs would often hire one of their waitresses to do the weekly vacuuming, scrubbing, and changing of sheets. The cleaning was supposed to happen on Mondays, after the previous week's comics left and before the new ones arrived, but sometimes it didn't happen until Tuesday, the day of the first show of the new week. It wasn't surprising to arrive at the club and see some girl in sweats, a university t-shirt, and a ball cap, dragging out a 32-gallon trash bag. Sometimes you can spot a waitress anywhere.

The furniture in these condos, more often than not, was rented, donated, or found at garage sales. The carpet would be tattered and littered with loose change and cigarette holes. The living room would have an industrial strength cloth sofa and chair, a coffee table covered in day-old newspapers and empty glasses, a lopsided aluminum floor lamp or a chipped table model, a picture of Elvis or one of those tacky city skyline photos, and a Samsung or cheaper RCA model color television. Comics spend an inordinate amount of their lives yelling at commercials, watching sports, and commenting on everything from the writing on "Sportscenter" to Lynn Russell's *fuckability*, as I once heard it described, so the television is the most important piece of furniture.

In the master bedroom, where the headliner slept, there would be a king-sized bed, a nightstand with a cheap clock radio, a dresser with at least one broken drawer, and its own bathroom. In the other bedroom, reserved for the feature act, you'd find a queen-sized bed, a nightstand, a cheaper clock radio, and a dresser, usually smaller than the one in the master bedroom, with more broken drawers. The feature would have to share a bathroom in the hall with the opener, who slept on the sofa in the living room. In Charlotte, at the Comedy Zone, they had a three-bedroom/one-bath apartment, so even if you were headlining, your room felt like a college dorm.

In these comedy apartments, a limited supply of linens and toiletries would be on hand, as well, plus the occasional sock, boxer short, or year-old *Hustler* behind one or two of the beds. The kitchen was stocked with mismatched plates and glasses and an occasional pot or pan. Sometimes the half-eaten burrito from Taco Bell would be thrown out of the refrigerator; sometimes it would sit leaking through the grates inside. The trash can would be overflowing with the remnants of 24-pack Budweiser's, Haagen-Daz containers, the occasional condom wrapper, and Domino's pizza boxes with one or two half-eaten stale slices of pepperoni still inside. Phone numbers of girls, food delivery services, local hospitals, and club management would either be scrawled on the front page of a ripped phone book or written on the kitchen cabinet itself. If there was a dining room table, it was one of thin glass or cheap pine.

I heard a story of a comic, a feature act, walking into one of these condos and seeing the headliner fucking some girl who was bent over the back of the sofa.

"Hey, how are you?" The headliner asked as he came over to the younger comic wearing nothing but a Steelers t-shirt and a hard on, "I'm Ted. This is Kami," Ted said, pointing to the girl bent over the sofa.

"Hi," said the voice. "How are you?"

"Fine," said the comic. "You?"

"Good."

One can only imagine what Kami thought about her life at that moment. Ted then showed the comic where the feature's room was, went back to the sofa, and then reentered Kami.

A club I was once working in Kansas City had filed for bankruptcy, but didn't bother to tell any of us who were scheduled that week; as such, we arrived on Tuesday to a condo that hadn't been cleaned in a month. As the week progressed, more and more of the furniture disappeared. We'd come back from the show on Wednesday and the microwave was gone. The next night, the TV; then the sofa. On Thursday, some, but not all, of the comedians' photos on the walls at the club had been taken off the wall. On Friday, there was nobody answering the phone at the club and all the utilities had been turned off at the apartment. It was a long, lonely Friday night drive home.

While we're in the area, there was a week's work between Manhattan, Kansas and Columbia, Missouri. Monday and Tuesday were in Manhattan at a club called Buschwacker's, and then comics would make the 300-mile drive on I-70 from the middle of Kansas to the middle of Missouri to finish the week at Déjà Vu, a club near the University of Missouri. I took Paul on this trip a few times, as he liked reading the road maps, eating the junior bacon cheeseburgers from Wendy's we had for breakfast, lunch, and dinner, going to movies in the afternoon, and hanging out in the club lounges at night eating popcorn and flirting with waitresses. Freddie DeMarco, who was one of the true three-dimensional characters in comedy management, ran Déjà Vu. He told a story about seeing a bartender and waiter scam him out of some money.

"My deal was that every time a waiter would get a pitcher of beer," Freddie said, "he'd give the bartender two bucks. Well, one time I'm watching at the end of the bar, and I see the kid put one buck in the register and one in his pocket. This goes on for a while: dollar in the pocket, dollar in the register. Then I see the fucking guy put both dollars in his pocket. I say, 'Hey, Tommy, what's up? We're not partners anymore?'"

Another great DeMarco story had to do with a woman he allowed to showcase on a Friday night. Sometimes, club owners will allow comedians to audition during a regular show. It's important, however, that this showcase doesn't go on too long, as it can screw up the evening, especially if there are two shows.

"I tell this broad to do five minutes," says Freddie. "What happens? She goes on ten, fifteen, and I see she's not getting off stage. So, I walked up to the stage, while she was performing, and dropped my keys at her feet. I told her, 'Lock up when you're finished.'"

One more. Freddie was well known in Columbia, so whenever he'd take the comedians out for lunch or dinner, everybody would stop and say hi to him. One Christmas he was at a mall with a bunch of comics and everybody was stopping Freddie to wish him well. Even the guy playing the mall Santa, with a kid on his knee, said hi to Freddie. One comic asked, "Hey, Fred who was that?"

"Hey, it's fucking Santa Claus. Who do you think it is?"

There's a joke about two comedians who are talking and one says, "Yeah, I worked this hell gig last week. There were only six people in the crowd, a toothless waitress spilled a drink on me, and the redneck manager didn't pay us until three in the morning. Plus, the hotel was a flee-infested pit, and to top it all off, the check bounced, and somebody stole my laptop from backstage."

The other comic says, "Yeah. Who books it?"

I worked a club in Amarillo, Texas, which was located in an old movie theatre. The first time I worked there, the club hired Wolfman Jack to headline. Problem was, Wolfman didn't have an act. He sat in a folding table, playing records and giving out autographs for an hour. The second time I was there, I worked with a girl who did rodeo tricks.

In Philadelphia, I worked a club that put the comedians at the Quality Inn, near the Betsy Ross Bridge which connects Pennsylvania to Jersey. At one time, a shooting took place in the parking lot. I was told by Cinnamon, a club waitress, not to worry. "It's not like the shooters were staying at the hotel or anything." Cinnamon, an economic honors student at Penn, has her breasts, navel, and clitoris pierced. "All the way down," she explained, forming a "V" with her hands.

One night, the air conditioner went out in the club, so after my set I took a walk on South Street through its vintage clothing retailers, piercing salons, tattoo parlors, gourmet grocers, art movie houses, condom boutiques, and, of course, Starbucks. There was a catalog in the window of the piercing salon that showed what one's scrotum and labia look like with hoop earrings inserted. Cinnamon told me a pierced penis actually increases the *woman's* pleasure.

On the street, I saw one couple connected at the neck by two spiked dog collars and a leash; there was a girl, no more than seventeen, on a bike wearing boxer shorts and sporting green hair; there was a woman in her early thirties, a gypsy, she insisted—sitting behind a card table in front of a pizza place telling fortunes for five bucks. There was a long line outside of Rosie's Water Ice. Traffic wasn't moving. A boom box was blasting from the top of a black Jeep Cherokee, and the cops were giving a ticket to some guy outside a restaurant called Three Hairy Sisters. I walked past the condom shop and wondered who would actually buy, cook, and then eat the penis- and vagina-shaped pasta that was in the window.

A half block from the club, I stopped at Satrbucks, ordered a chocolate something with whipped cream, and found myself next to a man who had his tongue, lip, nose and eyebrows pierced, a barbed-wire tattoo around his neck and forearm, and what looked like a steel rod impaled in his head.

I forgot to ask Cinnamon whose pleasure that increased.

Many clubs, in order to stay in business, gave free tickets to just about anyone who wanted one. It's called "papering" the room. An empty seat doesn't drink, so the more bodies in the club, the better. One way clubs give away these tickets is to hire telemarketers, so it wouldn't be unusual to arrive at a gig in the afternoon and see two or three puffy-eyed minimum-wage earners, sitting in the showroom, chain-smoking, eating fast food and talking on the phone. (If you're ever in a club that offers a chance for free admission, throw your business card in the fish bowl. You'll win. Everybody does.)

Usually, when a weeklong club put comedians in hotels, it was because management got tired of the upkeep of an apartment. Often comedians would punch holes in walls, steal microwaves, or allow candles to burn through the coffee table. Once in Tulsa, a comic spray painted on the living room wall, "This club is for loosers." (The club didn't fine him any extra for mispelling "losers.") If a comedian pulled the same antics at a hotel, the comic was responsible, not the club, so often management decided to find a Super 8 or Sleep Inn for us. These hotels were often located near a Denny's, Shoney's, or, if we were lucky, a mall, which is important because that's where comics spend a lot of afternoons. The hotel might serve a continental breakfast of plain donuts and containers of orange juice (some continent, huh?), which would save the comic some money—especially if we had sense to squirrel away a few donuts for lunch. The rooms in these hotels, while clean, smelled of too much disinfectant and cheap bedding; the mirrors hung too low to see much more than one's torso, the television would have limited cable, and the telephone would have a nipple red message light with a ringer loud enough to wake the guy in the next room and impossible to lower. In the bathroom, there would be wafer-sized bath soap, a half-ounce tin foil sheath of *Suave* shampoo, and small, thin white towels that reeked of bleach.

All of which is why I couldn't wait to stop doing gigs like these. Say what you want about Las Vegas, but working a showroom anywhere on the Strip beats doing comedy in a bar and staying in a motel in Starkville, Mississippi.

#!!°?)*%#*!( • ?#

If New York is the city that never sleeps, then Las Vegas is the city that can't. It's not unusual to see cocktail waitresses, still in uniform, playing video poker at 6:30 in the morning. Their faces—and outfits—tight from too much disappointment, alcohol and, judging from the foot-long franks in front of them, bad dietary habits. Weathered and aging hookers still walk the Strip, but they're not always looking for customers; sometimes they just need rides home. You can see old men in casino-affiliated hats walking purposefully through the gaming floor with seemingly nowhere to go. In the early morning, the best time to arrive and leave Vegas, the clanking of slot machines subsides somewhat and the full-price breakfast menus come back, replacing the graveyard specials.

Vegas is uncharacteristically quiet before the sun comes up and the smog arrives from Los Angeles. One is reminded that the mountains surrounding the desert are more impressive than the lasers, pirate shows, light extravaganzas and roller coasters of the Strip, but maybe that's because the attractions don't open till 10AM. Morning is the only time of day Vegas takes a breath.

Germane Greer once said of whichever city she didn't like at the time (Oakland, Tulsa) that there was no there there. In Vegas, there's too much of it. I saw a lounge singer once, his toupee too black and small for his head, wearing white shoes and no socks with a brown suit at the Maxim; I saw a couple from Tuscaloosa, with matching University of Alabama Crimson Tide t-shirts, each carrying a bucket of nickels, watching *La Cage* at the Riviera; I knew a cocktail waitress with an eagle tattoo on the width of her lower back and a boyfriend who had to wear a security ankle bracelet so the cops would know where he was; I knew a limo driver who ran a prostitution business from the bell desk and hit on all the comedian's girlfriends as he drove them to and from the airport; and, of course, I knew women with bad skin, who pierced their clits, nipples and tongues, dated abusive bar backs, did too much cocaine, and had too many children with too many different fathers.

The average stay in Vegas is four days, so people don't linger; neither do hotels. The Dunes, Landmark, Aladdin don't just close, they're imploded—as if they were being punished. The Forum Shops, at Caesars, is a mall for people who don't need one. Along with talking statues, there's a Spago, Armani, Dior, Bernini and other boutiques that are too expensive for anyone who actually shops in a mall. In other parts of Vegas, people beg for spare change, too, but there's none to be found. There are machines for that.

Most of my flights home left in the morning, and in the summer, with the hot wind blowing, the temperature could reach 101 degrees before breakfast, so I never left without my sinuses begging for mercy. My eyes were usually stinging from too much smoke and not enough sleep and that's when my thoughts turned to the lounge singer, the couple from Alabama, and the tattooed and pierced waitresses. This is a great place for documentaries. For all its excitement, Las Vegas is stifling much of the time. But you don't sweat here.

McCarran Airport always seems to be expanding. And the more I flew, the more the planes seemed smaller, the flight attendants older, and the middle seat passengers wider. And no matter how big or crowded an airport gets, sitting in a Taco Bell in an airport at this hour reminds you how lonely you are. When there's no one to drop you off, kiss good-bye, or even meet you at baggage claim, you find yourself rehearsing conversations with people who should have been there, once were, or promised to be again. I once saw a couple by a Haagen Dazs and marveled at how effortlessly they kissed, gazed into each other's eyes, and shared a mint chocolate chip ice cream cone. As I looked at the posters of happy people eating breakfast tacos, I wondered how my garment bag got so heavy and if I was really losing as much hair as the reflection in this napkin dispenser indicated. I was.

There used to be a man, a double leg amputee who was also missing an arm, who sat in a motorized cart outside Bally's, holding a casino bucket in his mouth, begging for money. His face was sunburned as only the Vegas sun can burn. He used to ride up and down the strip in his cart with a basket on the front covered in bumper stickers. I saw him every time I came to Vegas, and his expression never changed. It wasn't sad, wasn't happy, wasn't really anything.

Maybe that was the thing with Vegas. You couldn't see the pathos, frenzy and greed, and not feel a little superior to it all. This kind of perspective is not the same as insight, but sometimes it's all Vegas gives you. It may be all Vegas has to offer. It's a city of appetizers. You never go hungry; you never get full—no matter how many times you go back to the buffet.

The moments in Las Vegas lend themselves to metaphor; the lighting and contrast are better than most places. The tall black hooker with the overweight computer salesman, who comes for the Comdex convention every year, doesn't tell you much, but it's an absurd, wonderful image as they walk arm-in-arm in front of the exploding volcano at the Mirage. Joan Didion said that sometimes you run away to find yourself only to discover there's no one at home.

In Vegas, at least, you can get mint chocolate chip at seven in the morning and begin to understand why.

My first week of work in Vegas was at Catch a Rising Star, which was then at Bally's. I sent the agent a videotape of my show, and in theory, that's the way it's supposed to work. Only thing is, it's usually easier getting Elvis on the phone than it is an agent. The joke is that an agent goes to heaven and tells St. Peter that he was a good man, a good father, and a scrupulous businessman. St. Peter says, "Okay, well, great. Send me a tape."

The odds notwithstanding about an agent actually looking at a tape and calling the comic with work, we continue to send them (along with resumes, reviews, and self-consciously cute notes) and agents continue to stack them on their desks and use them to tape *Cheers* reruns. My submission to Bally's, however, was the only time it worked the way it was supposed to. The woman in charge of booking at the time, Winston O'Rourke, called me when I was working a club in Oklahoma City to say she enjoyed the set and offered me work. She said I would be helping *her* out if I could stay two weeks.

As I stood in the office of Jokers in OKC, writing down the dates, something told me to enjoy the moment. I had a feeling I'd never get a booking quite like this again quite this way.

I didn't.

Through the end of 2000, I performed over 75 weeks in Vegas—more than anywhere else in the country. Most of the weeks were at the Maxim Hotel, at a club called Comedy Max, but I also worked the Riviera, first at The Improv and then the Riviera Comedy Club, and the MGM, at Catch a Rising Star (after it moved from Bally's). I also worked the 4-Queens, which was downtown in the old part of Vegas, where you can still play penny slots and walk to pawnshops. One particularly depressing Christmas week down there, the 4-Queens offered free admission to attract people to the show. I remember performing in front of 18 mostly elderly widows that Christmas Eve.

"What brings you hear?" I asked a woman in the front row.

"My husband died this year and I couldn't stay in our home, so I came to Vegas."

As I said, a comic should never ask a question he doesn't know the answer to.

Compare a week on the 27th floor at the MGM, with its free buffet passes and tall cocktail waitresses in short black dresses to that of spending it in an Oklahoma City comedy condo, with brown ooze seeping out from the kitchen baseboard, and the brown-haired whacko who lived next door, and you can see why I was so anxious to get off the road.

Not that I didn't meet my share of brown-haired whackos in Vegas, including one woman, a sweet, troubled, accident-prone chemist from Ann Arbor, who said *amonymous* for *anonymous, probaly* for *probably,* and *pitcher* for *picture*. When she came to visit me at the Maxim, she slept in her jeans, shirt, and corduroy jacket. "Why is it so important we make love?" she asked. "Because," I said, "I'm too old to be sleeping with someone I'm not sleeping with." I know I ended on a preposition but I didn't think she'd mind—or notice.

There was also the time when I wound up in bed with three women, but one of them left because she felt guilty; another left because she felt left out. Thank God, one stayed.

Unlike hotels on the road, The Maxim's rooms had mirrors that made it impossible not to see yourself having sex.

It wasn't always pretty.

Since the hotels in Vegas fed us, it was possible for a comic to pocket his whole check, providing he didn't have a problem with gambling, drugs, alcohol, or women. No comic, of course, exists without one of those problems, so many comics left Vegas poorer than they arrived. There was a comic who used to work and book the Maxim and once won $25,000 on a progressive video poker machine, which, the joke went, put him *down* only $3,000 for the year.

The Maxim Hotel, before it closed down, had an advertising campaign, which said that it was "only steps to the famous Las Vegas Strip" and, apparently, real Vegas hotels. It was on Flamingo and Koval (across from Bally's), the same street where Tupac Shakur got shot in the head.

By the time I arrived, the Maxim's claim to fame, as far as I could tell, was that retired daredevil Evil Kneivel lived on the property. He was trying to open an Evil Kneivel museum, but the hotel, thinking there wasn't enough interest for an entire museum, offered a shop instead, next to the boutique. I think they settled on a shelf in the gift shop. I felt sorry for Kneivel as I watched him limp nightly towards the Cloud Nine Lounge. Once, he brought down a black box with skin care products. He rubbed some white goo on my face. "It's just like *Drakkar*, isn't it?" he asked. I wondered if a man like Kneivel, who was more famous than I would ever be, wound up living in a room at a shitty little hotel off the Strip, peddling his own line of cosmetics, what could the future possibly hold for an opening act at Comedy Max?

"Yeah, just like it," I said.

After the shows, comics would usually convene at the Cloud Nine Lounge before deciding where the evening would take us. We'd watch the local bands the Maxim could afford and the late night sports on a 19-inch television over the bar, bitch about the business, scam free drink tickets, and hit on women who had come to the show. Often, we would then go down to the Tropicana, Harrah's, Riviera, or MGM and hang out with the comics working those clubs and watch more TV, listen to more bands, scam more free drinks, and hit on more women.

The Maxim reserved three rooms for the comedians: 335, 337, and 339. These were the oldest rooms in the hotel and they had been passed over for not one but two renovations. Decorated in browns and oranges and featuring panoramic views of the Las Vegas strip, circa 1970s, they were full of stale, dead air, lopsided and chipped Formica tables, and carpets that had too many stains and not nearly enough steam cleaning. The rooms looked out the back of the hotel and at the kitchen air vents, so the windows, which couldn't be opened due to Vegas' fears that gamblers might do a half-gainer after a losing streak, were covered in a thick gray film. There was some talk that the cheap apartment complex down Koval housed nudists but the windows were always so stained I couldn't tell. One room, 339, was designated non-smoking, but that was routinely ignored.

A comic who worked the Maxim for years said that if the hotel ever thoroughly cleaned those rooms, they might find one or two feature acts. This is the same comic who, by his own admission, had a certain weakness for gambling, depraved women, and drinking; so, of course, he moved to Vegas. I heard that this comic was once on a plane that got bumped by a fuel truck as it was pulling into the gate. Nothing serious, but rather than wait for evacuation instructions, he ran through the aisle like George Costanza, throwing people back out of his way and back into their seats. He then climbed through an emergency window and jumped on the inflatable slide, which, unfortunately, had not been inflated. He broke both legs in the fall; consequently, he sued the airline. Supposedly, he won over $300,000, which he promptly spent playing horses, video poker, and flying deranged women into Vegas from all over the country.

You just hope a story like that is true.

I probably worked Comedy Max more than any other comic, but that wasn't necessarily because I was the funniest; it may have been that I agreed to go in as an opening act.

Most other comics, by comparison, might only get two or three weeks a year, but since I agreed to do the opening slot, I got as many as twelve weeks a year in two week blocks. It was an easy gig. I did 10 minutes up front, introduced two other comics, and made some closing announcements. As the years went on, though, it became more of a chore. Like many clubs in Vegas, the Maxim decided to sell its own merchandise, so after we comics came off stage, we'd stand behind a glass counter selling Maxim t-shirts and coffee mugs, as well as whatever the comedians had for sale. This included videos, cassettes, hats, condoms, fans, and fake eyeballs. On two occasions, the room in Comedy Max was also used for two topless shows: one called *Hell on Heels* and the other was a show produced my Michael Jackson's father. Glenn Hirsch, a comic, after seeing one of these shows, said, "Those girls do everything but yawn."

At Comedy Max, there were two shows per night and they only lasted an hour each. I got $1200 per week (less the 10 percent commission) and 14 buffet and drink tickets. It was steady, easy work, even if, as I said, it was an artistic dry well. As the years went on, though, the twelve weeks became eight weeks, which then became six, which then became four. Flying into Vegas for one week instead of two, staying at a hotel that looked like a set for a Divine film, and being the opening act in a club that had a cardboard cutout of the Vegas skyline on stage, became increasingly demoralizing. I would also work a week or two at the Riviera during this time, also as opener (I was told I was good at it), for about the same money. I was a Las Vegas comedian. It sounded a lot better than it was.

The kids used to come out to Vegas and visit during the summer or on winter or spring breaks. I'd get rooms with double beds and a roll-a-way, and we'd sleep late, eat free at buffets, spend the afternoons going to every hotel's video arcade, or just ride the tram between the MGM and Bally's. They enjoyed being known, especially at the Maxim, where everyone, including a bartender named Hollywood Tom, knew them. Paul learned to play nickel poker backstage one night from Connie, one of the waitresses, and Nina got to sit in a Vegas showroom and hear her daddy talk about her.

"Daddy," she once asked, "why do you talk about mommy on stage?"

"Honey, she was in my life, so she's in my act."

"Well, she doesn't like it."

One summer, while the kids and I were at the Maxim, Jane called and asked Paul if he wanted to come home early and go to a summer camp, which featured canoeing, horse-back riding, and camping.

Paul relayed the story to me later on.

"Yeah, Mom wanted me to come home, and she told me 'You sure you don't want to go canoeing? We could camp out, make S'mores. Come on what do you say?'"

"So what did you say?"

"Nah."

"You said 'Nah'?"

"Yeah, I'd really rather stay here."

"How come?"

"Because if I did that, I'd have to get up early, make my own breakfast, sleep in a tent. Who wants to do that when I can come here, play poker with Connie backstage, hang out with you, and eat shrimp at the buffet? Why would I want to go to summer camp, when I can come to Vegas?" he said.

"What did your mom say?"

"She doesn't like it."

Comedy Max had a maitre d' named—I swear—Cazzie Cazwell. Unlike many of those in the business side of comedy, Cazzie liked comedians. And while he wasn't actually in charge of Comedy Max, he cared more about the club than anyone else at the hotel. He'd wine and dine the vendors in town so they would sell more Comedy Max tickets and fewer tickets of other comedy clubs in town, he'd give comics comps to DaVinci's, the Maxim's fancy restaurant, when their girlfriends or wives came in, and generally, he'd promote the show anyway he could. He put up posters of famous comedians on the walls outside the

Comedy Max showroom, featuring performers from the '40s to the '90s, giving the impression that people like Bob Hope, George Burns, and Bill Cosby had played the room. In the '90s picture frame, he had a picture of Jerry Seinfeld, Jay Leno, and Nick Lewin, the Comedy Max afternoon magic performer. It was a gesture somewhere between sweet and absurd.

Cazzie, like Don, had been married more than any man, or two, for that matter, should. He told a story to Don and me once about his girl-friend who came over to his house to declare her love. "I mean, Jesus," Cazzie said, "you should have heard her: 'I love you, I want you' over and over. Christ, it was annoying."

"So what did you do?" Don asked.

"I told her to go, but then she said, 'Cazzie, I love you, I love you. Please.'"

"So then what?" I asked.

"What could I do?" Cazzie asked, "I threw her a fuck."

Don looked at me; I looked at him.

"He *threw* her a fuck," Don mouthed to me. "That's brilliant."

Towards the end of the '90s, my friend Kevin Kearney, who had been the manager of the Catch a Rising Stars in Philadelphia and Princeton, moved out to Vegas to book Catch at the MGM (once it moved over from Bally's). I worked a few weeks for him in '97 and '98, but then in January of '99, the MGM decided to throw Catch out of the hotel to make room for a Wheel of Fortune game show they were put-ting in. Kevin booked me in for that last week. Then MGM gave Catch a one-week extension, then another, and then another. Whether due to our friendship, my talent, or the fact that I was already there, Kevin asked me to stay all three weeks.

These extensions went on for the entire year, until the MGM final-ly closed Catch a week after Thanksgiving, but not until I had accumu-lated 20 weeks of work at that one hotel. I was still only making $1200 per week, but there was no commission, and I was working the MGM, *not* the Maxim. I was still the first act, but not the opener (Catch hired a musician who actually opened the show), so I got to do 30-minute sets. It was financially and creatively my best year in comedy, but I knew as soon as Catch closed, I'd be struggling again. I owe much to Kevin for that year, for it was a difficult one. My mom died in April of '99, but more about that later.

The eyes might be the windows to the soul, but in Vegas, you can tell more about a woman by her skin. Right below her eyes and above her mouth, you can see the residue of every illegal substance taken, broken promise experienced, blowjob performed in a hotel parking garage, and hour spent in a folding chair at an abortion clinic waiting room. I met cocktail waitresses, some successfully married with families, who had bought homes on the tips they made slinging drinks at Palace Station, but I also met girls in their 20's who were dating abusive bar backs, living in government housing with three or four children from three or four different men, and saving for boob jobs.

I once met a woman in her mid 30's at the Maxim, who said she had held some title of Ms. or Mrs. or Junior Miss Nevada. She also told me she had hired an illegal Turkish maid who eventually stole thousands of dollars and her soiled panties and returned to Istanbul in the middle of the night. Anyway, Miss Nevada (and who knows if this part of the story is true) said that in her 20's, she had slept with the likes of Jack Nicholson, Warren Beatty, Clint Eastwood and Michael Douglas. Imagine my good fortune, then, to get her in bed—at the Maxim no less. One night, in 339, the brown room (335 and 337 had the orange motif), we got to talking.

"Tell me," I said, "of all the celebrities you've slept with, who was the best?"

"Who do you think it would be?"

"I got to go with Nicholson."

"Well, you know, Jack's Jack."

"Okay," I said, "Jack's Jack." Like I knew what the fuck that meant.

"So he wasn't the best?"

"Nope."

"Well then—who?"

"Okay, you ready? Rich Little."

"Rich Little!? Are you kidding me? What made him the best: his ability to impersonate everyone else in bed? I can't tell you how disappointing this is."

"Why?" she asked.

"Why? I'd like to think that someday I'll make it big, and you'll be sitting in a bar somewhere saying, 'Yeah, I was with all the major celebrities: Jack, Warren . . . Barry,' but instead of being mentioned in the same breath with Nicholson, I find out I'm not even as good as Rich Little. What's the deal with his hair, anyway? He looks like Sam Donaldson."

"He's a great lover, I swear! But, listen, you're as good as Jack."

Being told I was as good as Nicholson was almost as flattering as having that University of Florida sophomore ask me to tie her up again in the Bahamas.

In many respects, Vegas had lost its glamour by the time I got there. The people didn't even seem attractive anymore. Some of the famous hotels had already closed, Sinatra was already singing from cue cards, and shorts and fanny packs were more popular than tuxedos and evening gowns. People buying commemorative shot glasses at the Harley Davidson café or watching *Riverdance* at New York New York were more numerous than the sleep-deprived, chain-smoking gamblers at the craps tables. Vegas was becoming Disneyland, or so it wanted America to believe, and if you didn't mind walking over adult magazines on your way to a theme park or roller coaster, I guess it was.

*I think Las Vegas needs a few more guys on the Strip handing out pornographic magazines. My son picked up one of those and said, "Hey, dad, do all women from Vegas have stars between their legs?"*

*"No," I said, "just the expensive ones." The cheaper ones have white-out. Some of these handouts have personal ads in them, too. One woman wrote that she was 5'1", 295 pounds and enjoyed biking. I'm thinking . . . not enough. Either that, or she's biking to Haagen Dazs three, four times a day. The ad went on that she was looking for a man with beautiful hair and beautiful eyes. Two of them? Should you be this particular at this weight? C'mon, it seems to me that if you're 5'1" and you weigh two ninety-five and a bald Cyclops asks you out, you go, girl!*

Where once people came to Las Vegas for the stars, they now came for the hotels. The people who build and own the new ones are like children arguing over who has the neatest toy. First, one builds a hotel that looks like a castle; then another builds one that looks like a Pyramid. Replicas of New York City (with a Brooklyn Bridge), Paris (with an Eiffel Tower), the Italian coast, Bellagio (with a dancing water show), and Venice (with gondolas and men well-rehearsed in broken English) dot the Strip. And now a casino based on the Titanic is planned. Dolphins and volcanoes and German magicians who make lions disappear draw more people to their shows than Elvis ever did.

The hotels, for all their varying themes, do have a certain similarity. Five minutes in even the nicest of them and you forgot which billion-dollar note you are helping to float.

As I said, my first gig was at Catch a Rising Star (then at Bally's). I was the opening act for a comedian/magician named Amazing Jonathan, whose act is designed to feature magic that doesn't always work. Even then, Catch ran only two comics per night and I did 30 minutes up front. Jane came out to see me that week, and we stayed in a junior Honeymoon Suite, complete with round bed and mirrors on both the ceiling and the wall. I noticed my name on the marquee was as big as the price of the Bally's "Big Kitchen" buffet. I was pretty impressed with myself until I heard Jonathan tell his agent that he would do Pat Sajak's late night talk show (this is when Sajak had one) but wasn't happy about it. Here I was content at having my name in the same size pica as a buffet sign and another comic was complaining about *having* to do national television.

I made $1100 that first week in Vegas (about what I made my last week) and while that wasn't the most money I ever made in comedy, it was in some respects, the most important. I wasn't working clubs in northwest Iowa anymore, where the smell of the meat packing plants kept me awake.

I was always anxious about coming to Vegas, though, no matter how many times I was booked. When I'd arrive on Mondays, at the start of the week, whether it was the Maxim, The Riv, or The MGM, I'd find myself rushing to the hotel's front desk, always afraid my reservation would be lost or that I had been cancelled.

In the early years I was just working Catch. I started working The Improvisation at the Riviera (The Improv has since moved to Harrah's and the Riviera now has its own club) a few years later. I had worked the Catch in Chicago, and after one of the shows, I went over to The Improvisation. The manager at the Improv, who had seen my act at Catch, told me to call the maitre d' at the Improv at the Riviera. When I got booked at Catch again, I set up a showcase.

So on a night in March, the night of the Academy Awards, I met the manager of the showroom at the Riv.

This is the part of any narrative where a brief description of the aforementioned character is fleshed out, but there is no easy, good, or succinct way to do that with Steve. Steve could be a tender, generous friend some of the time, an irrational vindictive bully at others. Trying to figure out which Steve was going to show up was part of the adventure in dealing with him. He remembered every slight (real and imagined) that he ever encountered. He told me he carried a loaded gun in his Jeep, but I also I saw him bring flowers to a dead girlfriend's grave on the anniversary of the woman's death. He blackballed comics for the flimsiest of reasons but worked another one four successive weeks so the comic could stay in town to be close to his dying wife. He could spend hours on the floor playing a game with his young daughter and then throw a table lamp at an employee who had the audacity to disagree with him. He had a way of making his friends feel both special and interchangeable.

Every comic who's worked Vegas has his or her own favorite Steve story. And there are as many comics as there are stories. My first meeting with him was one of mine.

"You know," Steve said at that first meeting, pushing his finger into my chest, "I don't usually stick around Monday nights, but I heard you were funny from that cocksucker in Chicago, so you better be good. You're going to do eight minutes up there. That doesn't mean seven, that doesn't mean nine. That means eight. I'm going to give you a one-minute light, and when you see that light, you got a minute to get off that fucking stage. If you don't, I'm going to rip your heart out right here. Got it?"

"Okay," I said. I hoped he was kidding.

This story is often repeated in varying forms by other comedians; one actually has Steve cautioning some comic, "Now, listen, I said seven minutes, not seven minutes and *ninety-nine* seconds; not six minutes and *ninety-nine* seconds. Seven fucking minutes. Remember!"

Most every comic who's ever worked for Steve also impersonates him because he seems so easy to do with his tough Italian guy persona, but he's not so much Vito Corleone as he is Sonny, who's tougher to do. Once, when I was in Princeton, Steve called and I happened to mention who I was working with.

"Oh, yeah," he said, "tell him to do me. He does an impression of me; it's pretty good."

"Steve, everybody does an impression of you."

Through the years, when the phone would ring, and I'd hear Steve's voice, my first thought would be, *What did I do wrong?* Being in a conversation with him was to be in a dance where you never got to lead. He doesn't ask for your opinion without first letting you know what he'd like it to be. Steve (who now plays Bobby "Bacala" Baccalieri on *The Sopranos*—what else?) put himself through college, spent time in Hawaii running a restaurant, and wound up in Vegas. He has a swagger that if you were seeing him in a movie, you'd think he was overacting. He doesn't so much take over a room as he tackles it. His weight fluctuates from the mere intimidating to the overwhelming. He knows his effect on people, and enjoys his ability to get away with it.

Once a customer complained to Steve about his behavior.

"You have been the rudest man I've ever met," the customer said, "and I'd like to talk to your supervisor."

"Go right ahead. Her name's Barbara," Steve said.

"And what's your name?"

"Steve."

"Steve *what?*"

"Don't worry," Steve said, "you just tell her Steve told you to *go fuck yourself*, she'll know which Steve you're talking about."

When I met him at Riviera in March of '91, he was only the maitre d', so he wasn't really in charge of booking The Improv. At the time, a woman, whose name I can't remember, was doing the job out of Los Angeles. A few weeks after my showcase, she called and said, "I don't know who you are, but Steve likes you and we like Steve to be happy."

I called Steve to thank him.

"She called?" he asked.

"Yeah, got work in July," I said.

"But she called? I mean, you didn't have to call that fucking cunt, right? She called you."

"Yeah, yeah. And I just wanted to call to thank you for setting it up."

"No problem, but she called you."

I told that story to another comic, who said Steve was in a good mood, because he doesn't always talk so nicely about the woman.

I liked working the Riv. There was a certain class of people who you wouldn't meet at the Maxim. It is where I met Duke University basketball coach Mike Krzyzewski. I had just finished a show and I was walking through the casino with one the Crazy Girls, the topless review at the Riv, when I saw Coach K playing dollar slots.

"Just want to say, I've always been a big fan," I said as I approached him. He looked at me kind of strange, so I tried again.

"You know, coach, I really admire your ability to run a clean program and the rate at which your players graduate."

Again nothing. I tried again.

"With so many programs under investigation, I think it's admirable that the Blue Devils have never been investigated. I think the integrity you've shown is admirable and classy." And, once again, he didn't say a word.

Then it hit me: I'm standing there in a suit with a girl from *Crazy Girls*, who's wearing cut-offs, a muscle shirt, loads of make-up, and hair piled up high. Here I'm talking about integrity and honesty and I look like I'm a businessman with a cheap whore. No wonder he was confused. But then I thought, hey, what's Mr. Integrity doing at the dollar slots at the Riv anyway?

It's funny what you remember when you're a comedian.

Once, at the Improv, a woman sat with her quadriplegic daughter. I could see them from stage. After the show, the woman came up to me and said her daughter was also blind, ninety-percent deaf, and severely retarded, but said she took her daughter to comedy clubs because, while the girl couldn't understand the jokes, she could feel the vibration of the room when everyone else was laughing. This, her mother told me, brought her daughter happiness. "The more laughter, the more vibration, the bigger the smile," she said. The mother then did a strange thing: she hugged me, and told me that if I ever thought being a comedian was a useless profession, I was wrong.

Thing was, I *had* thought that. The woman wasn't the only one crying as she left. I only wish I had been funnier so the room would have vibrated more than it did.

#!!°?)*%#*!( • ?#

In the beginning, Steve's job was to seat the three "Cabaret" shows on the Riviera's third floor—*La Cage*, *Crazy Girls* and The Improv (The Riv's main show, *Splash*, was downstairs, and out of Steve's domain.) *La Cage* was a show with female impersonators, *Crazy Girls* was a topless review where the girls did everything—as one comic said—but yawn, and the Improv, obviously, was the comedy venue. It was at the Improv where Steve had the most power. He was the de facto manager of the place. He told comics where to sit when they came in, what material to do, and whether or, more likely, how annoyed he was with one of us. While technically Steve didn't book the room, no comic worked there whom he couldn't tolerate.

He cultivated an image of himself as tough, mean, and unapologetic. He called comics from time to time just to "torture" them, as he would say, over something or other. He tested comics' resolve in every conversation, and only considered a few of them friends. The ones who'd brag about their friendship with him probably weren't. Once I overhead him tell a comic, "No one likes you, I don't even like you. The only reason you're here is that I threw you a bone, so don't bust my balls this week. I'm doing you a fucking favor. Remember that!" When the comic gingerly asked Steve why he wasn't in the first feature slot (The Riv has two), Steve responded, "See, that's exactly what I'm fucking talking about."

I never knew if Steve thought I was funny, but I was walking on stage once and he said, "Do that bit about your ex-wife fucking Bob. I love that."

Anyway, that first night, I did eight minutes exactly. The show went well, I heard laughs; saw Steve in the back smiling (or so I thought), and so I felt like I wouldn't be killed. As I was leaving, I noticed Steve had bootleg copies of the night's Academy Award winners on his desk.

"Hey, Steve," I asked as I walked out of the club to meet him, "I didn't know that tonight's Oscar winner had come out on video so soon, especially considering they're still playing in theatres all over the country right now!"

"Someone asked for your fucking opinion? " He said, smiling. Thank God.

"I heard that Joe Pesci just won best supporting actor for *Goodfellas* and in his acceptance speech, he thanked you for being his role model."

"All right, Barry, don't get too fucking comfortable." He laughed. We shook hands, and I went back to Bally's, met a girl from Oxnard, California, and wound up in the shower with her later that night.

As I said, it's funny what the mind remembers.

When Steve was still the maitre d', he'd meet comics for a brief meeting at 6PM on Mondays, the start of the comedy week, in the showroom. He'd give out the food badges that comics would need at the Riv's employee dining room, tell comics how much time they were doing and, most important, go over the rules for the week. One had to do with women and comps: "During the week, no problem, invite whatever skank you want, but on weekends, I don't want to see a set of parts in the club who hasn't paid."

He had a logic to life that wasn't so much understood by anyone as it was enjoyed or feared. Once, a comic came off stage and Steve met him at the end of the runway and said, "Hey, Willie, when did you start sucking cock?" Willie looked confused.

"What are you talking about?" he asks.

"Hey, Willie, your act. You're such a fucking liberal about this and that, and I notice you do little a gay bashing. Well, I'm fucking offended (He wasn't). I think maybe you could be half a fag. You know, covering up a little bit. Come on, you're sucking a cock, be proud. I know if I were sucking cocks, I'd be so far out of the closet, I'd be on the front lawn. So don't hide behind your act."

Apparently, Willie had once told Steve that one of Steve's comments about women, Orientals, blacks was offensive. And to be fair, Steve has a lot of offensive comments. No doubt, though, Steve found Willie's gay bashing material (and it was slight, but, again, to be fair, he had it in his act) hypocritical. Steve was maddeningly right about most of what angered him. He was hyperbolic and a tough love, but you wanted him on your side. No one I ever met read anyone faster or more accurately than he could. He also, if he thought of you as a friend (and no one ever knew for sure if he or she was considered one), could be wonderfully supportive and helpful. He made sure all his friends got to do *Evening at the Improv.* I know I wouldn't have gotten to do the show without him.

The Improv at the Riv booked four comics. I'd do eight or nine minutes up front. (If Steve decided during the week he didn't like the comic, he'd cut back the time. Once, he had a comic do three minutes up front.) The opener would then introduce the first feature act, who would do 12–15 minutes; then the second feature, who would do 18–20 minutes; and then the headliner, who would do about 25 minutes. Once the show was over, all the comics would stand behind a glass table, greet the crowd, and, like the Maxim, sell t-shirts and, strange as it sounds, condoms—*For a stand-up performance* the package read. The shirts were festooned with microphones wearing glasses, comedy brick walls, and the like. If a customer bought a shirt, and Steve was in a good mood, he'd throw in a condom for free. The proceeds of all this were not the hotel's, not The Improv's; they were Steve's. It wasn't that comics had to sell the shirts—there was nothing in the contract—but it was understood that it was part of the gig. Steve very rarely told an opening act to have a good show, but rather, "Sell shirts! Push the fucking shirts!" which the comic would do periodically during the show, often between introductions for the other comedians.

Most comics thought standing behind a glass table, selling merchandise a demeaning, needless exercise, but Steve didn't care. As the years went on, He got the comics an extra $50 a week for doing the shirts. It was a nice gesture, and almost made up for the indignity of yelling "shirts!" as the audience piled out of the showroom. Almost.

For the first year, I made $550 per week at the Riviera. Steve would give me five, six weeks a year, though, which made up for the money being so short. He always gave me the feeling he was doing me a favor, and, to a large extent, he was. There were many comics who would have worked Vegas for less money than Steve was paying me. I heard Steve say more than once about a comic, "You know, Barry, I did this guy a million fucking favors. A little ungrateful, right? Don't you think?"

"Right." I knew my lines.

As such, I never asked for a raise, but Steve slowly increased my money to $1100 by the end of the decade. It wasn't the money. There was something about the venue, something about him, something about Vegas that kept me coming back. Besides, I always felt a loyalty to Steve, even after it was obvious that he just thought of me as another comic.

He used to say that I was the "dumbest fucking Jew" he knew when, in fact, I was merely the poorest. Besides the shirts, Steve booked other comedy rooms in Fresno and later for Don at his club in Houston. Steve was once in a business that provided second mortgages to people who couldn't get them. Having him as a banker would no doubt cut down on late payments. He also had his own talent agency called Blue Diamond (for comics and bands), of which I was a part. I didn't ask to be represented; I just saw my name once under the Blue Diamond logo in an industry registry. The problem with having Steve as a manager is that he hated calling agents, club people, owners, in fact, anyone in the business. For a long time, he had an unlisted number—*and he was an agent!* "I am the anti-agent," he told me once.

A comic named Johnny Biscuit (no lie) once asked me to work a club in Provo, Utah. Due to its proximity to Brigham Young University, Biscuit asked comics to work especially clean. You couldn't even say the word *sex* much less describe any sexual act. I had worked with Johnny at the Maxim a number of times, so he felt comfortable with me working his club; Steve, however, didn't think I could work as clean as Johnny wanted. Should have been a simple deal, right? Club owner wants a comic and wants to pay the money, so agent makes the deal?

Not with Steve.

"Barry, you can't fucking do it. You can't be that clean. You can't talk about sex, masturbation, Bob fucking your ex-wife. You can't fucking do it and I told them so."

"But they want me!"

"You can't fucking do it."

Ten minutes later.

"All right, I got you the date."

"But I thought you said I couldn't do it."

"I don't think you can, but what the fuck. Do it. You get five for the weekend, a hundred for travel. Bring me back fifty."

He was right. I couldn't be that clean. Biscuit never asked me back.

I once saw him spend an inordinate amount of time helping a waitress with some menial task, and I asked, "Why do you bust everyone else's balls, but Miss Rhodes Scholar gets your Gandhi persona?"

"I got no problem with dumb," he said. Then, he saw a black man and a white woman walk by. He immediately joined his fingers together, mimicking the promotional piece for the Spike Lee movie *Jungle Fever* and asked, impersonating Rodney King, "Can't we all just get along?"

Another maitre d' we all knew at the Riv once asked out a waitress, who not only had a questionable reputation, but also was rumored to be a pretty heavy drug user. Steve asked where the guy was planning to take her, and when the guy said to a movie and then for some ice cream, Steve exploded.

"Where... for what? Don't waste time! Give her a shot of heroin and bring her back to your room."

I could never decide, though, whether he believed all of what he said or just did it for effect. I would see him with his wife, his babies, and he could be Alan Alda—albeit Alan Alda on a bad day. He once took me to The Forum Shops at Caesars so I could help him buy his wife a Mother's Day gift. As he left the mall with a Mickey Mouse watch and a $200 gift certificate for some running shoes, she called him on the car phone to see where he was. She must have asked something like *What are you at the mall for?* and instead of saying, *It's a surprise* or *You'll see* like a normal husband, Steve answered, "For none of your fucking business, that's what for."

Later that year, he agreed to re-take his wedding vows. He told a bunch of us that night at the Riv that he tipped the priest in advance to keep the ceremony short. He impersonated the priest during the ceremony, at first shunning the money, but then taking it. "'Oh, no, I can't take this,'" Steve said, quoting and mimicking the priest, and then adding, in his own voice, "Fellas, up went the vestments and the three twenties went right in his fucking pocket, and all the time saying he was saying "'Oh, no, Steve, I couldn't.'"

Steve's most colorful takes, though, were on women.

"Other than my wife, and a couple of old friends, I really don't like them that much."

Once, standing at a bar at the Maxim, Steve saw a woman he casually knew come towards the two of us. She was smoking, frowning, and had gained 20 pounds and what looked like 20 years since he last saw her.

"Oh, this isn't good, Barry. What a broken down cunt, huh?"

"You know," I said, "most people would have gone with *broken down* or *cunt* but not both."

"You think?" he asked, smiling. "Well, what would *you* call her?"

He told me a story about a comic who met a girl in Vegas and how the two liked talking dirty to each other.

"So," Steve says, "this guy is fucking her and he says, 'I'm going to fuck you, I'm going to fuck you,' and the girl's saying, 'I want to suck your cock,' when the guy says, 'I'm going to fuck you like a whore.' Well, then, the girl snaps. 'What did you say?' she asks, completely breaking the mood. The comic's a little confused, but he says, 'You know, the thing we're doing with talking dirty.' The girl then says, 'Did I hear you right? Did you say what I think you said?' The guy is getting real fucking nervous now, and says, '"Yeah, but you know, you and me, the thing: *I'm going to fuck you, I'm going to smack your ass . . .* C'mon you know. It's what we're doing.' The girl then says, again, 'What did you call me?'"

By the time Steve finished telling that story, which concluded with the girl leaving the comic naked in bed, Steve had me in tears.

He hated women who cheated on their husbands; he hated men who did the same, but understood it more. There was a story in Vegas about a guy who came home and found his wife in bed with a maintenance man. The husband snapped, killed his wife and the guy, and was now standing trial for double murder. As we comics gathered around Steve after a show, he leaned back in his folding chair, and said, referring to the case, "Can you imagine what that must be like? I mean, you break your fucking balls, working 10, 11 hours a day and you come home and your wife is fucking some plumber. I mean, this husband must have snapped. He couldn't have been all there anyway. I ain't saying what he did was right, but I can understand how you see something like that—your wife fucking some guy—and then you cut her up into little pieces and shove her down the fucking drain. I'm not saying I would do that, but I don't know if I'd vote to convict either."

Thing was, there was nothing in the paper about the guy cutting up his wife into little pieces and shoving her down the "fucking" drain.

Steve continued:

"Boys, listen to Uncle Stevie. If you ever catch your wife sucking some fucking guy's cock, or just fucking him, here's what you do. You shoot her first; then you shoot the guy. It's important you do that in order. Now, this is important. You then go outside and break the window from the outside in—not the other way around. This way, when the cops come, you tell them, 'Hey, I saw this guy on top of my wife; I thought he was raping her. I went crazy, I reached for my gun, I guess I shot them both by mistake.' The cops'll look around and see the glass and think the shine broke in." Steve now points to his head. "Now, don't forget, break the window from the outside in. If you do it the other way, cops ain't going to find no glass in the room and they're going to think something's up."

After Steve finished the story, a comic, Billy Elmer, asked, "Just how much thought have you given this?"

The greatest compliment I ever heard him give a comic was "He makes me laugh." He almost said it apologetically. But when he didn't like a comic, he could be equally succinct. To one, a notorious thief, who was in the showroom to watch a headliner Steve liked, he asked the offending comic, "Hey, Joey, what are you doing ... shopping?" He told more than one comic to dust their "acts off" when he felt they weren't writing enough new material. Then there was the story of the gay comic, who was in town to put together a gay comedy revue. The comic was thinking about naming it the "The Gay Freedom Tour." "What kind of name is that?" Steve asked. "Name it what it is: something like 'A Couple Cock Suckers Telling Jokes.'"

He once told a Chinese couple in line to see The Improv that they wouldn't understand it and to "go see *Crazy Girls* next door." When they insisted that they wanted to see comedy, Steve said, "No, you want to see tits." And that's where they went. Another time, Sandy Hackett, son of Buddy, had opened a club at the Stardust Hotel. It didn't last long, and one night Sandy came over to the Riviera to see Steve.

"Steve," Sandy said, seeing the sold-out line at The Improv, "how do you do it? I've got no one at my club and you filled the place. I don't get it."

At that moment Steve saw two Chinese women walk by strolling a baby carriage.

"Sandy, your problem is you don't have a hook. You need an angle, a marketing strategy. See (pointing to the Asians) it's 'Chink baby night.' Bring an Asian baby, get in free."

In all the time I knew him, I rarely saw Steve have a moment of self-doubt. I always imagined that dead girl, the one who got flowers from him, must have had some pull on him, but I never asked. Alan Alda you could ask; not Steve.

Through the years, I worked for him mostly as an opener, but once in awhile, he'd move me up to the middle slot. That I was headlining everywhere else in the country impressed him very little, so I didn't push to be moved up. I was happy to get the work. He then started booking the acts at the Maxim (Conflict of interest, you say? C'mon, it's Steve. You tell him). In my life, there have been a half dozen people who, no matter how secure I thought I was, could make me feel like I was nine years old again. Steve is at the top of the list. Often he'd begin the conversation with, "Barry, look, you're a friend of mine . . ." I knew trouble was about to follow. I also knew, even during the best of times with Steve, the friendship—or whatever it was—wouldn't make it until the end of the decade.

It didn't.

It ended in 1999. I had been booked to work the Riv a week after my mom died. Kevin, at the MGM, called and said to come back to work whenever I wanted. I asked for a week that preceded one I had already scheduled at the Riv. I was bringing my father to Vegas and wanted him to get out of Jersey for a couple of weeks. Now, to be fair, Steve had a rule, which he often let slide, that comics couldn't work different hotels in successive weeks. When I called him and told him about my mom and the week at the MGM, I expected him, considering the friendship, to bend the rule. Wrong. He told me he couldn't change the policy (he could; he had before), and that I would have to choose between the MGM and The Riviera. Since I had my dad coming out the week I was at the MGM (and since I thought Steve was being an asshole), I chose it over the Riv. We never spoke again.

One more story: and it has to do with Frank Sinatra. Steve knew Sinatra, not well, but well enough to once be invited to his house in Palm Springs. Steve told me he called his wife from Sinatra's Palm Springs living room and said, "Guess whose fucking house I'm in?" Anyway, when Sinatra had his 75th birthday party in Vegas, Steve was told he'd get an invitation. It never came; what he got was a call from one of Sinatra's people telling him to just come by the Desert Inn, where the party was being held, and hang around the bar outside the ballroom. Once Sinatra knew that Steve had been overlooked, he'd be invited in; but Steve would have none of it. With him, you either get an invitation, kick in the door if you have to, but you don't stand around, schnorring your way into a party—even if it is Frank Sinatra's 75th birthday.

## CHAPTER 10

# My night on the Titanic

I promised my daughter I'd get her Leonardo DiCaprio's autograph at the post Oscar Titanic party in Beverly Hills. Personally, I just wanted to see Kate Winslet's tits.

Unfortunately, DiCaprio was in Europe, promoting his new movie, the one where he plays himself *and* his evil twin. There's a story circulating out here that he might be gay, which devastated Nina. Paul broke the news to her.

"He is *not*," she said. Take it back."

Ah, if only life were that easy.

As for Winslet, when she arrived, she didn't look happy. Her breasts were on my mind, not because I'm a breast man—I'm not—but because I had heard she had gained gobs of weight and that her tits were starting to sag. From what I could see, she wasn't playing soccer with them, but they weren't exactly perky. The movie isn't as cute if poor little Leonardo sinks to the bottom of the ocean while the love of his life grows up to be Delta Burke.

*I hated this movie. First of all Winslet looked old enough to be DiCaprio's mother. What were we watching anyway? Titanic or The Graduate? She was like Mrs. Robinson, for Christ's sakes. And while we're at it, it would have killed Winslet at the end of movie to scoot over a little on that broken door so Jack could have hopped on? All the guy did was save her life. Move the fuck over, you selfish bitch. And what's with the song? My heart will go on. Huh? You're dead; I'll love again. Thanks for the nude drawings. Ba-bye*

I only got a chance to be at this party because my brother, Wayne, who writes for *The Hollywood Reporter* (he's now with *Adweek*), received an invitation for two. He wanted to take Monica, his new wife of five months, but she was talking to their marriage counselor and didn't want to miss the session.

Don't ask; it's L.A.

As Wayne and I, dressed in suits but not the tuxedos required on the invitation, drove in his 1988 Suzuki down Canon Drive, I noticed perhaps a hundred people behind barricades, waving and gawking at every car that drove by. They waved and gawked at us, probably thinking we were celebrities who were making a statement by driving a shitty jeep; we waved back, pretending they were right. Such is the thirst for celebrity out here on Oscar night that we could have been delivering linen and gotten a round of applause. Two valet attendants opened the embarrassingly lightweight doors of the Samurai, and we proceeded down the red-carpeted sidewalk, which led to a converted tent-covered parking lot that housed the party. As I walked past the crowd, we got even more waves.

"Fuck, we really should have sprung for the tuxes," I said.

"What do you mean we're not on the guest list?" Wayne asked the three women checking in guests at the front table.

As it turned out, we weren't. Fortunately, a guy who knew the guy who invited Wayne got us in, but not before a woman with reading glasses perched on her nose told me to button the top of my white shirt. "It'll make your suit look more like a tux," she said, not smiling, checking off something on her clipboard.

"Christ!" I heard her mutter to herself as she walked away.

To be at an Oscar party is to understand why the rich are sometimes shot in the head during Third World coups: little Titanic-shaped salmon and caviar appetizers were being served.

We arrived long before the important guests but right after the caterers. The Oscar broadcast, simulcast on three large screens, had just started, but few were watching. People with nametags and walkie-talkies walked through the empty tent, talking to other people with nametags and walkie-talkies. Wayne and I circled the floor and watched the food come out. At one table, I grabbed what looked like a leftover Hamantaschen from Purim, but then I got a stern rebuke from the woman in charge of the pasta. "We're not serving yet, sir." She let me keep the pastry.

As Wayne and I leaned against a make-shift booth in the center of the floor, a woman, a Meg Tilly-type, in a pretty but tight red floral dress, came over, smiled, undid my top button, patted my chest, and told me I'd look more important that way.

"Fuck it looking more like a tux," she said, "you're fine."

She stayed for a few minutes, but when Wayne mentioned that he was a writer and I a comedian, she left.

"Hey, Wayne, you know the joke about the Polish actress who fucked the writer?"

"No."

"She was never heard from again, so do me a favor: don't tell anybody else what we do for a living."

The guests started arriving. I saw Bill Maher, from *Politically Incorrect*, dancing with an exotic, tall Asian woman. Jeffrey Tambor, best known as Hank on *The Larry Sanders Show* (but for me he'll always be the gender-ambivalent Alan Wachtell on *Hill Street Blues*), was going into a portable bathroom as Tom Arnold, inexplicably left out of Oscar consideration for his work in *The Stupids* or *Carpool*, was coming out. Drew Barrymore, or someone who really wanted to be, was talking to two Italian girls who didn't speak English—at least not to me. I smiled at Anne Ramsay, Oscar winner Helen Hunt's sister on *Mad about You*, as she walked around, alone, chain-smoking and eating cookies.

Wayne then found some people he knew, so I strolled around the tent like a prom date left alone. I saw the Italian girls, still with Drew, but now sitting with another woman in a leg cast. When I asked the

Italian with the small tits if I could buy her a drink (They were free; that was the joke!) she looked at me, squinted, looked at her friend with the big tits, and said nothing. Nothing—not a nod, a smile, a wink. I must have been invisible.

I tried again.

"Can I buy you a drink?" I asked slowly, as I mimed drinking.

She looked down, looked up, looked down, and then pointed to her drink.

"Have."

That's all, no pronoun, no *thank you, anyway*. Just *Have*. I redid the button on my shirt, and went for another Diet Coke. I saw Jeffrey Tambor and told him how brilliant he was in *Hill Street*, citing his line on cross-dressing to Captain Furillo. "You're a beautiful and sensitive man, Frank, but you have a lot to learn about gender re-identification."

"You really do know the show, don't you?" he said, "Thanks." He moved away quickly.

Tables towards the back of the tent were reserved for James Cameron, his wife, whom he'd soon dump, and a few others, most notably Sumner Redstone, Rupert Murdoch, and Celine Dion. Solemn security men guarded their empty seats. A woman, a paralegal from Paramount, along with her friend, explained something about Fox giving Paramount $65 million to finish the film, but that was okay, she said, because even though Fox got the video rights, Paramount still got the better deal because they got the domestic distribution and a percentage of the international gross. I nodded like I knew, cared, what she was talking about.

Later, Wayne asked how my conversation went.

"We have to set our heights higher than a Paramount paralegal and her dumpy roommate. This is big time, Wayne, and if we're going to be shallow, let's be shallow and humiliate ourselves in front of really important people."

He agreed.

Other VIP's started arriving: Juliana Margulies from *ER*, Kim Delaney from *NYPD Blue*. Wayne thought he saw Sharon Lawrence, also of *NYPD Blue*, but wouldn't swear to it, or what she was doing now even if he did.

"Behind you," Wayne mouthed three times before I turned and saw Jay Leno with a woman (his wife, Mavis, I guess), drinking champagne at one of the tent's four bars. I'm a comedian, I thought, he's a comedian. Here's my chance to network. But he moved away before I could run out to the Suzuki, get an audition tape, come back, and embarrass myself.

Then, like they were let off a flatbed truck, wafer-thin model-types started arriving—bitchy and gorgeous, tall and implanted, they came in hordes wearing black dresses and blank stares. They were either on the arms of men with carefully cultivated and coiffed stubbles or bald, dumpy men with good tans. But they did not come alone.

When *Titanic* won Best Picture, there was much applause, but even more relief. The movie was no longer just about it's budget, authentic china, and really hot male lead; it now had credibility. It was now art.

The longer I stayed, the more I thought about Chinese food and sex, and how neither is ever as good as anticipated. If we're all six degrees of separation away from power and wealth (not to mention Kevin Bacon), then tonight, all the degrees were here. It was the entire depressing schematic: the studio heads, stars, mistresses, character actors, arrogant statuesque freaks of nature, paralegals, women in charge of pasta and pastry, women with clipboards and reading glasses, and brothers of advertising writers.

It was clear why the Italian girl dismissed me. Who was I to ask her anything? Would Mira Sorvino really have anything to do with Quentin Tarantino if he were still peddling videos at a Hollywood Blockbuster instead of *Pulp Fiction* at Cannes? Would Tommy Mottola have left his wife and family for Mariah Carey had she been working at a Best Buy instead of being the highest-selling female recording artist of all time?

Sex, real estate, and status—location, location, location.

With all the limos waiting to leave, the valets were going to take their time getting to the Suzuki. As I walked outside, most of the people behind the barricades had gone home, but I noticed Celine Dion, flanked by two beefy security men with earpieces, coming in.

*Don't worry, Celine, your seat is safe.*

The Paramount paralegal told me Celine (like they were on a first name basis) was wearing the $2 million necklace from *Titanic*. But if I remember correctly, no such heirloom existed on the ship; still, there it was: a gorgeous, fictitious heirloom, now protected, dangling from her neck. Hollywood at its best—life imitating art's imitation of life.

And I never got to taste that fucking salmon.

## CHAPTER 11

# Where are you, Neil Diamond, when I need you?

noticed on the clearance shelf at B. Dalton a pictorial retrospective on the life and career of Neil Diamond. The back cover, complete with a resplendent Diamond, his hair plastered down like a Klingon from the original Star Trek series (or maybe like a young Sam Donaldson), proudly proclaims that for many, Diamond is the "King of Rock." Were Elvis really dead, I'm sure he'd turn over in his grave. (Actually my favorite Elvis joke was told to me by Bobby Sessions, who said that he had heard a rumor that Elvis' favorite board game was Scrabble: "I have trouble," Sessions said, "with the thought of Elvis, sitting around Graceland, saying (and this is where Sessions did a pretty good Elvis) 'Sonny, Red ... is Nuttybutty one word?'") Anyway, the thought of Diamond as the "King of Rock" confirmed that not enough people had seen *The Jazz Singer* or listened to "Heartlight" all the way through. Next to the Diamond book, there are discounts on assorted Dick Francis novels (Doesn't this guy ever get writer's block?), self-help hardcovers on cholesterol, finance, and relationships, a retrospective on the MTV *Unplugged* series, an autobiography by golfer Craig Stadler (*I am the Walrus*) and two coffee table collections: one called *Dolls*; the other *The Jews*. (A book on the Jews discounted for Christmas. Now that's funny.)

I am at the mall today with my children. It's December 23, and time to get their mother a gift. I don't usually take them for their holiday shopping this early, preferring to wait until Christmas Eve, but I've got to be in Vegas on Christmas Day. We're at Things Remembered (but I'm sure this gift won't be) and they've decided to buy, and then engrave, an empty 18-ounce perfume bottle that looks like a wine carafe. The purchase made, Paul and Nina run off to the arcade, leaving me (and the carafe) to walk through the mall. Everyone looks horrible. My mother once wondered how it was that with all the money spent on fashion, so many people looked like shit. Looking around, I see lots of yellows, reds, and lime greens and remember what my friend Francesca (remember: the vibrator named Picasso?) said about some fashion being a privilege, not a right.

A couple, in matching shiny teal nylon jogging suits, attempt to take their son up the escalator in a stroller. There's an elevator they could have used; on the other hand, how often do you get to see the cracks of two fat asses in one viewing? There's a large woman with her large kid sharing a small popcorn by the indoor merry-go-round. She doesn't look like she can afford the buck for the popcorn, much less the buck-fifty for the 90-second ride.

Some days, especially during the holidays—*this* holiday—people seem to be moving at dizzying slowness. They stop their cars at yellow lights; they stand still on people movers. They're like cassettes that stick in a tape deck.

I have no idea what Christmas is supposed to feel like, but this can't be it. There's an assumption in Oklahoma that everybody is Christian or just one good witnessing away from becoming one. When you're a stubborn Jew, this can make for a long December.

When we were married, Jane rarely went to church; I rarely went to temple. Religion only seemed to matter when we saw the other one take an interest.

*I'm Jewish; my ex-wife is Methodist. So we had plenty of money, we just didn't know how to enjoy it. But being Jewish in Oklahoma is difficult. I put on a yarmulke; Okies think I'm stealing a salad plate. Plus, there's Oktoberfest, which you may like, but when you're Jewish, the thought of Germans in a tent drinking beer makes us Jews a little nervous.*

As I got older, Judaism began to matter to me; as such, it mattered to me that it mattered to the kids. Jane, too, has become more religious, and since she has custody of the kids, she gets first pick on the holidays. The kids and I always celebrate Chanukah, even though I always have to borrow a menorah from Ed and I still don't know the third prayer that's required on the first night. Once, during Kol Nidre, Nina was so moved, she cried during the service. I took it as a personal victory. Ed and Anita always invite us over for Passover, and, when Nina was little, she liked asking the customary four questions. Paul, ever my son, tried to parlay the holiday into a day off from school and an excuse to drink the Manishewitz.

On Easter and Christmas, Tulsa is very much a Christian town—proud, quiet and closed. Even the always-open Albertsons isn't.

Some Sunday mornings, I drive by the Village Inn and see well-dressed families in hard shoes getting out of their cars; I drive past the 60-foot praying hands at Oral Roberts University (erected, I imagine, to complement the 800-foot Jesus he once saw), past the glorious Boston Avenue Church downtown, and past the gaudy Golden Driller statue by the Exposition Center—even he looks Christian. The few cars I see on the road are filled with people, sitting tall and proud. Jews, as a rule, never get dressed up for breakfast.

There's a joke about man named Izzy, a Jew, who takes his $2 million fortune and goes to live on a deserted island. Soon he gets lonely, though, so he has a $900,000 temple built; a few weeks later, he takes his remaining $1.1 million and has a slightly fancier sanctuary built.

Years later, his best friend comes looking for him, and seeing the $900,000 temple, says to Izzy, "That's a beautiful temple, my friend."

"Yes, it is," says Izzy, "it's where I pray."

Then, the friend sees the other sanctuary, and is even more impressed.

"My God, Izzy, now *that* temple is exquisite."

"Yeah, well, let me tell you something," says Izzy, "you couldn't pay me to walk in there."

Anyway, the reformed rabbi in town (and, yes, even though Tulsa only has 2,000 Jews, it, too, has two temples—one reformed, one conservative) told me once that even Moses wasn't such a good husband, so I shouldn't feel so bad about my inadequacies. He also said that the Jewish bible makes no mention of Jesus; as such, we don't even have a record of Christ ever existing. "Even the term *New* Testament connotes that it's an improvement over the *Old* Testament, which is what we Jews study—and it's not. They have their bible; we have ours."

This should make us many new friends.

My ex-mother-in-law told me one Easter that the Jews were forgiven for killing Jesus a long time ago, so she had no hard feelings towards us. The conservative rabbi in town, who told me he was a big fan of Sam Kinison's, mentioned how it's considered a double mitzvah to make love on the Sabbath, which raises the interesting question of whether it's a quadruple mitzvah to sleep with two women on the Sabbath. He said only if you're married to them both, and, of course, since we're Jews, not Mormons, that's not an option.

In the best of times, being Jewish in Tulsa is like being a guest in someone's home—welcomed, respected perhaps, but always a visitor. During the holidays, it's suffocating to see the off-duty policeman directing traffic by area churches, the little girls in their white dresses and matching shoes playing in front yards, the crosses made when office buildings leave lights on that run down and across its façade, and the *Jesus Loves You* greetings from the girls at the Wal-Mart Superstore, which, thankfully, is never closed for too long.

#!!°?)*%#*!( • ?#

I bury my hands self-consciously in my pocket and walk past the Food Court, filled with too many people and too many packages, past the Body Shop, filled with fragrances made in an animal-safe environment, and past a cosmetics counter at Dillard's, filled with ones that aren't. The stuff at Dillard's smells better. I don't go by the arcade because the kids will want more money, so I go to Mr. Bulky's, instead, and buy some red and green M&M's. So what if they cause hemorrhaging in laboratory rats? They're tastier than the brown ones.

As I stand outside in the cold by Sears (my hands in my pockets now for a reason), I see the parking lot is full—even the handicapped spots. There are three teenagers on one bench sharing a pack of cigarettes; a girl, with a face full of acne and very pregnant, sits alone on another, waiting for a ride.

I go back inside and back to B. Dalton. A tall, thin woman with caramel hair, dressed in black, and smiling to herself, is leafing through a *Men are from Mars, Women are from Venus* sequel. She reminds me a little of Asia.

> Men are from Mars, Women are from Venus? *Let me get this straight: Women are from Venus, planet of love and passion; Men are from Mars, planet of dust and gas. What . . . the title* Men have their Heads up their Asses *was already taken?*

This girl is mesmerizing. I watch her read, flip the pages back and forth, and play with her hair. I want her; I want this moment. In my mind, we could go to Vegas, make love on an Egyptian-themed comforter at the Luxor, ride the roller coaster at New York New York on New Year's Eve and then go to this tacky bar at the Peppermill, sit around a fire, and be served frozen drinks by women in long evening gowns. She'd laugh if I told her any of this; still, as I pretend to read about the section where Neil Diamond decided to do the music for *Jonathan Livingston Seagull*, I notice she's looking in my direction. Is she thinking about sex and drama and frozen drinks, too, or, like so many women I've met on the road, just wondering why I'm staring at her?

> *Quick, put the book down. You don't want her to catch you reading about Neil Diamond.*

Too late. She's leaving. She smiles, sort of, pulls a strand of hair away from her mouth, walks past the 1997 calendars and into the mall. I smile, but she's already gone.

I could tell you I went after her, tell you I saw her at Abercrombie and Fitch buying a knapsack, tell you what I said, how I flirted, how she laughed at the ant and elephant joke, how we met for cappuccino, and made out in front of the Foot Locker. I could tell you we spent the next few months in bed until her abusive ex-boyfriend came back into her life and how I lost touch with her until I got a postcard from Spain telling me she was pregnant or dying of cancer, but none of that happened

Instead, I went to the arcade and gave the kids another few bucks each. But first I finished reading about Neil Diamond's acting career.

Did you know Olivier never wanted to do *The Jazz Singer* with him?

## CHAPTER 12

# I, Claudia

laudia had been coming to the Bahamas with her father, mother, and brother since she was an infant. Her dad had made millions selling auto parts in Europe and, like many wealthy Germans, found the sun of the islands to be a welcome change from Germany's evil weather. After Claudia turned 18, she started coming by herself and would usually rent a condo at Paradise Harbor Club, a resort near the airport. She played professional tennis as a teenager, so often she'd play in tournaments at the exclusive Ocean Club and, after winning them, sit topless on its private beach and drink Mexican beer and read American novels. She had actually gone back to Germany the week I met her, but said Germany was too depressing in the winter, so she came back. And she brought a friend.

I first saw her standing outside Joker's Wild, when the hotel was still owned by Merv Griffin, and the club was in the part of the Beach Tower that's now The Seagrapes Buffet. She and her friend were both looking at the pictures of the comedians on the placard by the door. I could see them through the glass.

"Richard," I asked from inside the club. "Who are they?"

"German girls. Be careful."

I walked outside. "Say something encouraging before I go on stage," I said to both of them.

"Beautiful," the shorthaired brunette said, pointing to the picture. She kissed me on the cheek. "Better in real life."

That one turned out to be Claudia, so, naturally, I asked out the other one, Petra.

We went to Rock N Roll by Crystal Palace in Nassau. As Petra droned on about her plans for the future, I watched Bahamian men, shirtless in white drawstring pants, dance with American girls in denim skirts or sun dresses. I also watched Claudia, who came along with us, sit by herself at another table, smoking, drinking Diet Coke, and reading *The World According to Garp*.

She was dating a bartender at Rock N Roll when I met her. She was 22; I was 36, and divorced from Jane a year and a half.

A few days after my date with Petra, on the Monday between shows, she and Claudia invited me to their condo at the Paradise Harbor Club for dinner. I was sitting on the sofa when Claudia walked out of her bedroom, through the living room, and into the kitchen. There was something about her walk, the way she moved her shoulders and ran her hand through her wet hair; the way her shirt and jeans fit on her body, the way she smiled as she walked by, and even the way she lit a cigarette. By the time she started making the salad and gently dancing to something on the CD, I was in love with her. And I knew my life would never be the same.

I told you: the Bahamas will do that to you.

After dinner, the three of us went to Columbus Tavern, the restaurant and bar at Paradise Harbor. I made sure that I sat between them. Once again, Claudia was quiet and Petra wouldn't shut up. Claudia was wearing a sweater vest over a gray t-shirt, which I assumed was uncomfortable, so I reached into my sparkling water, a drink, up until that point, I had never ordered in my life, took out an ice cube, and began rubbing it on her neck.

"You look hot," I said.

Petra looked confused. I held the cube against Claudia's neck and saw drops disappear down her back.

"You know, if you saw *9 1/2 Weeks*, you have to pop that in your mouth," she whispered.

It was the first full sentence she ever said to me.

"You know, if *you* saw *9 1/2 Weeks*, you have to come get it."

I hadn't seen the movie, so I have no idea if that's what she was supposed to do; still, I put the ice cube in my mouth. She looked at me, smiled, and then kissed me, slightly opening her mouth. I pushed the cube back into her mouth with my tongue. I ran my hands through her hair; it was still damp. I could feel Petra staring. I didn't care. I felt Claudia's tongue push the cube back in my mouth. She then put her fingers to my mouth; I kissed them. The bartender was smiling.

"We're going to get in trouble," she said and kissed me again.

"Another water, sir?" the bartender asked.

"I have to see you again. I don't care how embarrassing this is."

"Hey, what's going on?" Petra asked.

We ignored her.

"I have a boyfriend and, worse, Petra looks very upset," she said. I quickly kissed her again.

"I *have* to see you again." I said.

"No, great!" she said after a few seconds. "My whole life I watched other people have moments like this. My whole life, I'm usually the one sitting where Petra is."

The next night she lost her virginity. But before we made love, before I lifted up her olive green t-shirt and kissed her breasts, we sat on my $7^{th}$ floor balcony, eating two-dollar Mounds bars and drinking three-dollar cans of ginger ale from the service bar. Claudia was smoking—she was always smoking—and sitting on the balcony and smiling at the stars around the moon. We watched a late evening buffet being torn down by the pool and listened to the thud of Bahamian music coming from one of the local bands. Lit by the hotel, the ocean appeared to be running sideways and the sky was unusually wide. There, on plastic chaise lounges, life had both a view and a soundtrack.

"Was good, yes?" she asked the next morning.

"Yes, the best ... ever."

*So how many guys have ever made love with a virgin before? I did and I don't feel I'm betraying a confidence by telling you this, because I told her I was going to tell everybody I met. Anyway, it was wonderful, but she had a lot of questions. She said, 'Barry, I don't know anything about sex, so what else do you like? What else is normal?' 'Look,' I said, 'those are two separate questions. I'd like you to strap this on and wake up your roommate but I don't think that's what you're asking.'*

As she was showering, I listened to the jet skiers on the Atlantic Ocean and the construction workers on another wing of the hotel. There was an uncharacteristically cool breeze coming in through the sliding door that led out to the balcony. I lay there in bed, wondering how to freeze time.

As I heard her sing something in German over the spray of the water, I could imagine us living in New York City and having a child, whom we'd name Chloe. I also could imagine a time when Claudia would leave me and America and go back to Germany, where, I feared, she'd die in a car crash or on a street late at night. I thought Chloe would have her mother's eyes and be raised by Germans.

"What are you thinking about?" she asked, as she jumped, naked, on the bed, and stood over me. I noticed a tiny mole above her breast and a scar below her knee. Her body was tanned and wet and she was smiling. I smiled back.

"I think you're going to be trouble."

"That'll teach you to start with ice cubes."

I remember buying donuts and condoms that week on our walks into Nassau, eating conch salad in Styrofoam bowls under the bridge, which we called Heart Attack Bridge, at Potter's Cay, putting suntan lotion on her mole, and watching her smile at me from the back of

Joker's Wild. I remember sitting on the patio of her condo at Paradise Harbor and eating cashews from a jar and asking her to join me on the road for a string of one-nighters in northern Florida and southern Alabama; I remember driving in a rental car outside of Tallahassee while she ate double bacon cheeseburgers and tried to read a map of Florida; I remember sitting in a hotel in Ozark, Alabama, and watching her write postcards to her friends in Hamburg while she sat topless in jeans; I remember thinking that a week earlier this girl was a 22-year-old virgin from Germany and now she was watching *SportsCenter* in a Fort Walton Beach, Florida, hotel with a Jewish comic; and I remember flying back to Miami together and saying goodbye in a terminal between my connection to Tulsa and hers to Nassau. We had lots of good-byes through the years. We got good at it.

A week later, she called.

"I've decided you shouldn't be alone on your birthday, so unless you want me not to come, I'll be in Las Vegas on your birthday."

"What time does your plane arrive?"

A month later, we were in room 339 at the Maxim in Vegas. She rented a red Miata, played Roulette, wrote our names in one of the marquees on the wallpaper, and, for my birthday, laid out 37 roses on the bed.

"I bought them from a man at the Excalibur."

"A *man* at the Excalibur?"

"Yes, I took the car out of valet, drove up and down the Strip, looking for flowers for your birthday."

"You keep this up, you may get me in bed."

"Good," she said in a high-pitched voice. She was impersonating Dan Patrick.

The next day, we went to Bourbon Street, which is across the parking lot from the Maxim, to pick up the car.

"Why didn't you bring it to the Maxim's valet?"

"Sweetie," she said, "I'm a twenty-two-year old German, who

recently lost her virginity. I just flew 112,000 miles to see you. I couldn't find the Strip, I couldn't find the flowers, I couldn't find the hotel, and, besides, all these hotels look the same, so don't bust my balls. And why do you make everything so difficult in this country?"

You have to love a girl who will say *Don't bust my balls.*

"Why do we make things so difficult? 'Cause we won the fucking war," I said. "Had you Germans won, you could have done things your way, but since you didn't, we're in charge. We can put valet parking wherever we feel like it, we can hide the flowers, and we can take advantage of young German girls if we like."

She gave me the finger.

I taught her how to play Keno and what to order in a kosher delicatessen; she bought me German chocolate from Ethel M's at the Fashion Show Mall and gray shorts at Just for Feet. We took the red Miata and drove to Hoover Dam, where we didn't wait in line to see it, and then to a matinee of *Schindler's List,* where we did.

"Did any of your family die in the camps?" she asked after the movie.

"None that I know of."

"Is your family very religious?"

"Hitler wouldn't have cared," I told her. "Let me ask you something: What did *you* think of the movie? I mean, being German."

"I think Spielberg was too easy on us; I really do. Why didn't I know about Schindler?"

"There were many Schindlers; there were just many more Nazis.

"I can't get that little girl's red coat out of my mind," I continued, "just seeing it on that burning pile of clothes."

"I think," she said, "for me, it was the beginning: when those people sat around the table with the candle. It was like they were talking to the dead."

"In a sense, they were," I said. "It's called Kaddish."

"Sweetie, I think it was a good war for you to win."

Later that summer of 1994, I went to Germany for the first time. In Hamburg, Claudia lived in a rundown, industrial part of town, which wouldn't even be worth noting, but her family had made millions in auto parts, so she could have afforded something much better, but she said she liked the way that part of the city woke up each day. I think she also enjoyed annoying her father by living this way.

On the first morning of my first trip there, about six months after we met in the Bahamas, she drove me in her black Peugeot to Berlin. The Wall had been torn down a few years earlier, so we took pictures of Japanese tourists taking pictures of a church. We ate Whoppers on the grounds of the Reichstag, bought German t-shirts that read *I want my Wall Back (only this time 3 meters higher)*, looked at the makeshift crosses erected for those shot or impaled trying to escape the East, and got a parking ticket.

Later that same day, we went to the concentration camp at Bergen-Belsen (I played Otto Frank in a college production *of Diary of Anne Frank*, and since Belsen was the camp Anne had died in, I wanted to go there.) Claudia bought a history book of the camp and I noticed how the memorial stones in the welcoming center made no mention of Jews. I wrote in the register set aside for guests:

"A Jew from Oklahoma and a German from Hamburg visit here five decades later and are falling in love. Maybe the good guys won after all. Barely, but won."

As I kneeled in the mud by one of the mass graves, Claudia came over and crouched next to me.

"A lot of these people never got to yell at shitty German waiters," I said, "or be in love or complain about how angry the weather gets in this country."

"You blame me?" she asked.

I smiled because for a moment I thought she was asking about the waiters and the weather and didn't see her pointing at the grave.

"Why would I blame you?"

"Isn't there something called 'collective guilt' that we Germans are supposed to have?"

"What do you know about collective guilt?"

"I know enough to know you know about it."

"You know, there are people who say that every Jewish baby born spits on Hitler's grave," I said. "Maybe our being here does the same."

"Then we go home now and make love. And do more spitting." She grabbed my hand, helped me up, and draped her arm over my shoulder as we walked back to her French car. The car's CD player came on as she started the car. As she backed up over the gravel parking lot, I remembered, again, what my grandfather said about music and cemeteries.

"Sorry," she said. Surrounded by mud and tears and restless clouds and souls, she turned off the stereo. "No time for sound."

My grandfather, who left Poland before his country became a Jewish graveyard, and who surely would have been in one of those graves we were kneeling over had he stayed in Ludz, would have liked this girl.

We flew to Mallorca, Spain, a week later, where her parents had an 11-room home in the hills that overlooked the Mediterranean and a yacht, *Gemini Lady*, named for Claudia and her mom. Claudia and I drank bottled *agua sin gas* (I loved ordering it in Spanish) and Greek espresso in cafes, swam nude in the pool that overlooked the Mediterranean, and tried not to crash her dad's SL500 on the narrow roads on our drives into Palma.

One night, after we made love, she noticed the condom had broken inside her. We sat on the bathroom floor and peeled the pieces of latex out of her and thought of baby names.

It's a strange place to discover that you'll never be more in love.

I left a week later to go home. Seemed like one of us was always leaving.

#!!°?)*%#*!( • ?#

She came back to the Maxim on New Year's Eve, where I got to kiss her on stage while strangers applauded. When we got back to the room, she had two pizzas and two two-liter Diet Cokes waiting for us. We woke the next morning and turned on the television and discovered that 400,000 people had been on the Strip bringing in the New Year.

"It seems like we missed a party last night," I said.

"Hmmm, any pizza left?"

She left the next day to fly home and start graduate school.

I walked back to the hotel from the airport and had a feeling that no other year with her would ever be as good. Two months later, I was lying in bed at the Maxim, right under "our" marquee at around 9AM when the phone rang.

"Sweetie, wake up," she said in an accent more German than it needed to be.

"We won the fucking war. I don't have to."

I don't know what we talked about for the next nine-and-a-half hours, but I remember we broke up.

"You're the only thing I think about," she said, "but you can't be. Sometimes, I just want to be a 23-year-old girl."

"Listen," I said, as I struggled to get dressed—by this time, it was fifteen minutes to show time—while keeping the phone to my ear, "you will always be the most-loved girl in Germany."

"I didn't think I could be this happy if I lived five lifetimes," she said.

Later that night, between shows, I met a short blonde in a short black dress at the Rio. She came back to the Maxim with me, and as she stood in 339 and lifted her dress to her waist, told me I was the most beautiful man she had ever seen. Later, while I was on stage during the second show, I saw her sneak out. This was also the night at the Cloud Nine Lounge when Evil Kneivel rubbed his personalized cologne on my face. In a day that I could have otherwise skipped altogether, it was oddly the perfect ending.

## CHAPTER 13

# I, Claudia Part II

hings ended, but they didn't stop.

I returned to work Joker's Wild a few days later, a year to the day that I had rubbed an ice cube on the back of Claudia's neck. It would have been one thing had the memories stayed quiet, but they appeared to be hanging from the palm trees in front of the hotel. I thought of her when I walked by her old condo, thought of her when I went over Heart Attack Bridge to Dunkin Donuts to get a Boston Cream, thought of her when I used the "say something encouraging" line to women looking at my picture outside the club, and thought of her when I slept with the women on whom the line worked. She was in every lounge chair that lined the pool, every accent I heard on the beach, every shop on Bay Street, and every broken-down taxi that passed by. She had changed the landscape. Paradise was now effort.

She called that week and said, "I don't think I can ever rest my head on anyone else's shoulders for the next 20 years . . ."

She was like wrestling with someone who kept going up in weight class.

Ernest Hemingway said that Marlene Deitrich could break your heart with just her voice. Claudia was like that. I'd like to think what made her voice so hypnotic was its struggle to articulate all that passion, disappointment, anger, and love inside her, but maybe it was just raspy from the Winstons. Whatever it was, it disarmed me. Often, she seemed to be speaking in subtitles, and somewhere between the German and the English, she would lose her concentration—or nerve.

Maybe I endowed that vocal struggle with too much; maybe it wasn't love or wisdom. Maybe it was just the accent.

When she'd call, there would be a delay before I'd hear her voice, a delay filled with echoes, purrs, and the unmistakable crackles of international connection . . . I'd know it was Claudia. The ring even sounded different.

Later that summer, she asked me to come visit. The circus was back in town.

So, I went again—in August of '95. This time, instead of staying in Hamburg or flying to Spain, we took an Inter City European (ICE) train to Austria, where her parents had bought a home—this one in the Alps, near Kitzbuhel. I was going to ask Claudia to marry me on the train, but I knew she'd say no; so, instead, I joked with her about her smoking habit and our cabin boy we named Igor and his secret Nazi past.

"You think he knows I'm Jewish?"

"Sweetie, even if you weren't, he wouldn't like you."

Somewhere south of Munich, I looked at Igor looking at me and then at the perfectly planted and curious alignment of German trees that bordered the tracks. Claudia was smoking, of course, and listening to 10,000 Maniacs on her Walkman. I could smell the air conditioning coming out of the vents at the base of the window.

Theodore White once wrote that song in Germany was different from song anywhere else because of its rhythm—something about its primordial beat making it possible for total German strangers to lock arms in bars and sing and dance and toast and kill Jews. So, too, I thought, was there something different about their rail system. To stand in their cavernous stations, as I did at Hamburg's Hauptbahnof before the trip, and see and hear German trains is unlike doing so in New York's Penn Station, watching the Long Island Rail Road. To smell the diesel fuel, see the German skinheads drinking American beer, and hear the garbled loudspeaker is to know that the past and present, for all Germany's protestations, live comfortably here.

I looked at the people in the station that day and wondered who among them were there fifty years ago when the trains and tracks were used to haul cramped and frightened people to prison and death. A man about 75, picking his nose by an upstairs railing, was watching the trains come and go. He is old enough, I thought, to have done the same thing in the same place in 1941. Even today, between its overpriced McDonald's and underweight heroin addicts, echoes still compete for attention in Hauptbahnhof.

Maybe John Calvin Bachelor was right when he said that the sins of the Nazis will be around for at least five generations and that the forty years since World War II had been but one ejaculation.

I wanted to share this with Claudia, but the rocking of the train had put her to sleep. I took out a photo album she had brought along.

"What are you doing?" she asked. The turning of the plastic sheets in the album had awakened her.

"Sorry. Looking for the unsavory element in your family."

"Try my mother's side," she said, and then went back to sleep.

Even over the noise of the train, I loved the sound of her voice.

When she woke, I watched her read an international edition of *Vogue.*

Claudia wore only blacks, whites, grays, and olives, and rarely wore makeup. In all the years I knew her, she didn't own a tube of lipstick or pair of pantyhose. Wearing jeans, a t-shirt and a baseball cap, she looked like a teenage boy. Her eyes, brown with a touch of green around the upper edges, were big and young, but when she smiled, they rarely looked as happy as her mouth. Her hair was silver now. She was a brunette when we met, but she went blonde, caramel, and then shaved it off completely before dyeing it silver. In her teens, she had hair down to her waist, but cut it above her shoulders because she tired of people telling her how lovely it was. She was exquisite—even if I couldn't tell you why and never knew what she'd look like when I'd see her. I also never knew what tense to put her in. She danced in and out of my life so often I had to change the narrative when thinking about her. Ours was a story with a beginning and many ends but no middle. It was love without a net.

"You haunt me." I told her.

"*You* are the only man I will ever love."

Claudia was my Sybil, the woman with the multiple personalities. I sent her Sybil's autobiography as sort of a half joke, and wrote on the inside flap, "I love you. All of you, as many of you as there are."

She thought it was a sweet thing to write.

Her parents' house in Kitzbuhel overlooks a place called King Mountain, and in the distance, I could see ski lifts climbing the ascent as houses and property values inched skyward. Her parents spoke some English, but I spoke no German, so Claudia had to translate the conversations. In Spain, the previous year, she did this willingly, but here in Austria, I could see her tiring of it. I knew that she wasn't telling me everything they said.

"I don't know what they do to me," she said one night in bed, "but sometimes I wish it would go away. I wish my dad would stop drinking himself to death and my mother was one of those big moms with big tits who would wrap her arms around me and let me cry, but that's never going to happen."

"Then why do you keep coming to see them?"

"I love them. Why wouldn't I? I keep thinking it'll be different, but it's impossible being their daughter. You never know whether any success you have is yours or theirs. My father's accountant once told me I would never have to work a day in my life; my children wouldn't have to, and neither would my grandchildren. I don't want that and yet I let them fly me around, pay for my apartment and school. I'm a hypocrite."

"Why don't you divorce them?"

"Can you do that?"

"You make Claudia happy," her mom told me a few days later. "A lot of boys have tried, but I know my daughter. She's a Gemini. Remember, *Baddy*, she has two personalities."

"I wish it were only two."

As Claudia and I sat on a balcony that night, we heard Don McLean's "American Pie" coming in the window from a neighbor's party.

*I met a girl who sang the blues, and I asked her for some happy news.*
*She just smiled and turned away.*

"That's you, you know," I told her.

"What do you mean?"

"You're the girl who everyone wants to make happy."

"Why do you want to?"

"It has something to do with the way you walk across the floor of a Bahamian condo."

We sometimes talked like people in a short story.

"I think before, when we make love, if you're not wearing a condom, we'll get pregnant," Claudia said, "and then we name after the father."

"Bad luck." I told her, trying to figure out whether she was talking in the past, present, or future tense.

"What do you mean?" she asked.

"In the Jewish religion, you're not supposed to name a child after someone who's living—only someone who died."

"I don't understand."

"Some Jews believe," I said, "that after a person dies, the angel of death comes for his or her soul. If there are, let's say, two Barrys in the household, the angel might take the wrong one by mistake. That's why Jews give children a name that honors the dead but won't confuse the angel."

"That's so beautiful and goofy at the same time. What kind of God would allow that kind of mistake? Are his angels really that stupid that they wouldn't know who is to die?"

"You're asking me about the stupidity of angels? I don't know. Some things you take on faith."

"Fate?" She asked.

"No, faith."

"What's the difference?"

I didn't know.

"I guess faith," I said, "is having an irrational feeling that something will happen but you can't explain why; fate is having the same irrational feeling something will happen but you can't explain how."

"Are we about faith or fate?"

I didn't know that either.

"I only know that if there's a God, and he cares about stuff like this, he'd have opened the ceiling that first night we spent together in the Bahamas, and said, 'Don't fuck this up; you two will never be this happy again.'"

"How do you make me laugh and cry like that? You really think God would say 'don't fuck this up'? What kind of poet are you? My whole life I thought about you. I want someday for your children to teach ours about the difference between gray and blue skies. Part of me, Sweetie, could die right now and not feel like I missed any of my life. You're going to be loved forever."

"I just hope I make it till December."

On my last day in Austria, I was alone on the same balcony and looked at the mountains surrounding Kitzbuhel and thought about White, Hemingway, and Don McClean. I thought, too, about Claudia and all the cultural, historical, and vocal voices in my life at the moment. Claudia was in another part of the house, reading a German Economics text book; her parents were drinking beer underneath a Cinzano umbrella on the patio; and I stood with one of the two dogs— the big black one who limped—watching a woman walk a cow in the fields below and bare-chested Austrian men deliver a sofa.

That night there was no music coming in from the windows.

"You think you'll ever get married?" I asked, knowing *we* never would.

"Who would have me?"

"Well, whatever you do, never trust a guy whose hair doesn't move."

"And you never trust a woman in white stockings—unless she's a nurse."

"Sometimes I see you in a big loft with a guy named Heinrich. Maybe he's a poet; maybe a German house painter."

"Too messy—all the cans and brushes around."

"What about the poet?"

"Also too messy. What about you?" she asked.

"I had a crush on a Vegas Keno runner once."

"We fuck in their honor." She laughed.

"Yeah, but the secret is knowing when to fuck, when to make love, and when to know which it is you're supposed to do."

"I don't think there's ever been a time with us when there wasn't at least a little love."

"Maybe more than a little."

"Keno runners, you only fuck, okay? Never love. Promise me? Nothing will ever come as close to this."

Promise.

"What do you want on your gravestone?" She asked, as she brushed my hair from my forehead.

"What!?" I laughed. I realized she wasn't joking. "I don't know. I think something like 'I knew this would happen.' How about you?"

"'She tried.'"

## CHAPTER 14

# The first half of 1996

et me go back a few years. Two nights before my divorce in 1992, two nights before I spent it with the girl with the two vibrators, I was working the Laff Stop in Austin.

And I met Yvette.

The first thing I noticed about her—the first thing anyone would notice—were her eyes. Teal, wide, and very white, they were alive and unforgiving.

She was at the Laff Stop because she knew the other comedian. After the second show, he had invited me to join them for a drink at the club's bar. I don't drink, so while they threw down Crowns and water, I refilled my own Diet Coke from the soda gun. He then said he was going to Sugars, a topless club nearby, and would we want to go. Yvette didn't, which I think upset him. I guess he assumed she would enjoy watching strippers in ankle boots and cowboy hats grab dollar bills out of his mouth with their tits. I didn't want to go, either, mainly because Yvette wasn't going. If she was staying, I was, too. After he left, though, she said she was going home. I quickly muttered something about the power of her eyes and my sudden urge for a bagel and a Dr. Brown's Black Cherry soda. We wound up at Katz's Delicatessen in downtown Austin. We then went back to the Comfort Inn, where we sat out by the pool, and talked about her work as a paralegal and my work as a comedian.

"Did you see my set?" I asked.

"Yeah, but, sorry, I don't remember it."

(I'm not sure any woman who's ever loved me thought I was funny.)

Within a week, we were in Vegas at the Riviera. In the months that followed, I'd fly down to Austin at least once a month, usually on a Friday, and we'd go to Pizza 'Nizza, sit outside, and argue about acceptable pizza toppings; on Saturday mornings, we'd walk to Whole Foods and buy bagels and 24-packs of Coke, and then on Sundays, we'd sit naked on the sofa and watch football or *Firing Line*—I figured William F. Buckley would enjoy that.

Yvette would make lasagna on Sunday afternoons, painstakingly removing the olives from my side of the pan. Don, who knew Yvette from the many trips we took to his club, told me one time, "She's going to kill you if you don't start eating those fucking olives." After dinner on these Sundays, Yvette and I would split a pint of Cherry Garcia yogurt and then go to 6<sup>th</sup> Street, where I'd watch her drink. It was at a club down there, over a urinal, I saw a piece of graffiti.

> *Just remember guys. No matter how good-looking she is, somebody, somewhere is tired of fucking her.*

"Just let me know beforehand, okay, Barry baby?" she asked.

She loved nature, animals—*critters* she called them—and Crown whiskey; she also had a strong right jab.

On a trip to the Bahamas, a few months later, she told me about a man she almost married who was so abusive, he once stood over her with a gun and threatened to blow her brains out.

"I forgive him now," she said one day on the beach. "In fact, he's one of my best friends."

"I couldn't forgive someone who did something like that to me."

"You don't understand, Barry baby."

Later that night, after six or seven Crowns and water at a club called Crocodiles, she said, "Who are you to judge my life?"

"Huh?"

"About Joe. He's changed; he beats himself up every night over that, and if I can forgive him, I don't need your approval to have him as my friend. And who the fuck are you to judge anyway, considering what you've done with your life?"

It was a nasty argument that went on for most of the night. She wanted to make love; she wanted to find a flight home to Austin. In the morning, after the Crown had let go, she apologized, but I remembered what someone told me once about no woman ever being improved by alcohol.

"You know what bothers Jane most about you?" she asked me once.

"That I live and breathe?"

"Only partly. Your fights aren't always about you."

"What do you mean?"

"The reason she always seems annoyed is because that's what happens to a woman who wakes up every day next to a man she doesn't love. Women like Jane get angry with the person responsible for putting them in a position of unhappiness, which, in this case, Barry baby, is you. Had you not fucked up her life, she wouldn't be with Bob."

During the two years we dated, Yvette was faithful; I was not. She never asked me if I was, so I never told her I wasn't. She was supposed to join me in the Bahamas when I first met Claudia, but she had to cancel at the last minute. Had she come that March in 1994, I never would have been sitting at Columbus Tavern, kissing a girl in a sweater vest—at least that's what I told myself.

Did I juggle the two of them? Yes and no. Claudia knew about Yvette; Yvette didn't know about Claudia. When I thought about the story of my life with the two of them, Yvette was the narrative; Claudia was the parenthetical. When I finally told Yvette, I was working the Laff Stop in Houston and staying—you guessed it—at the Allen Park Inn. We were no longer dating. (For that matter, neither were Claudia and I.) Yvette came up to see me from Austin anyway, and, somehow, we wound up in bed. While we lay there after the second show on Friday, watching television and eating hamburgers, I asked if she had dated anyone since we stopped seeing each other. Big mistake.

"No. I was seeing a guy, but it only lasted a month. How about you?"

I don't know why I decide to be honest when I do, but I told her about Claudia: the meeting at Columbus Tavern, Claudia's loss of virginity, the trips to Germany and Vegas, the red Miata, everything.

Yvette cried, threw shoes and a right cross at me, and threatened to return to Austin.

"I feel like I just found out my husband was cheating on me."

"But I wasn't your husband. That's the point."

"No, the point is, you lied—the one thing I asked you not to do. I didn't ask you not to fuck anybody; I asked you not to lie. And I asked you not to lie so I could be a part of whatever it was we were doing. You were not in this relationship alone. In some ways, you're worse than Joe."

"Worse than Joe?! You compare what I did with Claudia to a guy standing over you with a gun at your head?"

"I didn't *love* Joe."

"Look, how was I supposed to tell you I met a 22-year-old German virgin in the Bahamas on a trip you were supposed to be on?"

"How about this? 'Hey, Yvette, I fucked around on you with a young girl.'"

"Everything about Claudia was surreal. I never thought I'd ever see her again."

"But you did."

"Yeah, and every time I did, I thought it would be the last time. And when it finally was the last time, I really didn't see the point in telling you."

"So why are you telling me now?"

"I don't know."

"Do you still love her?"

"No," I lied.

"Tell me something: what do you talk to a 22-year old German virgin about?"

"I don't know," I lied again.

"Barry baby, you ripped my heart out." And then we made love.

After everything I told her, she still loved me—right up until the time I made another trip to see Claudia.

Which brings me to the first half of 1996.

#!!°?)*%#*!( • ?#

The first Sunday after New Year's, six months after that trip to Houston, four months after I went to Germany to see Claudia and two months after she told me she loved one of her roommates, I was in my apartment with a former girlfriend, Marie, when Yvette called to say what a *fuck* I was. Ten minutes later, with Marie still in the apartment, Claudia called to say, "I hate my world. Can I have yours back?" and asked me to meet her in the Bahamas in a month. It took me about 12 seconds to agree, but another three hours to get off the phone, during which time, Marie left.

And then...

Two days later, I was working the Houston Laff Stop again. And I saw Asia. We had kept in touch after my divorce, so I knew she had moved to Houston, but I had never called her. Why I did on this trip, especially considering how 48 hours earlier I made plans to meet Claudia in the Bahamas, I don't know, but Asia and I met for dinner at a place called Birraporettis. We sat at a tall table and ate calamari and ravioli, and talked about ants, elephants, Joan Didion, Asia's boyfriend, and Claudia. Asia came to the early show on Saturday night, but said she had to leave before I finished my set. To get to the stage at the Laff Stop, you have to enter from the side runway adjacent to the bar. Right inside the showroom are two doors, and it is against those, that I kissed her—in view of 250 people.

"I've wanted to do that for, oh, six years. And now I don't think I ever want to kiss anyone else," I said.

"Do it again," she said.

I'll be late for work. Besides people are staring at us."

"Can I stand here and watch?"

When I came off stage, she was still there.

"I thought you had to leave," I said, as I grabbed her hand and walked through the bar.

"I do, but you owe me about six years worth of kisses, you know that?"

The next morning around seven, my phone rang.

"Hi, it's Asia. Can I see you today?"

"Yes, sure."

"Then open the door."

When I did, she was standing there, talking on her cell phone.

I remember two things about that morning: she was crying and my phone was ringing. I knew the call was from Claudia; Asia's tears were about a 57-year-old flight instructor (she was 23) who hadn't touched her in eight months. I couldn't imagine ever getting tired of making love to her, but maybe the grafitti on that bathroom wall applied to even girls like Asia. I know I should have felt guilty, what with Claudia and all, but if Claudia was one of my three great loves, then Asia was one, too. You make space for the great loves in your life even when there isn't room.

A few days later, when I got back to Tulsa, I found a letter from Marie taped to my door and packages from Claudia, Yvette, and Asia. Claudia had sent me a CD of a German folk singer, Yvette had returned two shirts I had given her years before, and Asia, recalling a fantasy I told her about, sent a pair of panties and red-handled scissors. That night, around 11:30, Marie came by carrying a television she had promised me. She also wanted her letter back. Marie and I had dated in early 1995, between Claudia and Yvette (though both were still on my mind) but it had ended in the summer of that year—peacefully, I thought. In the letter, though, Marie told me how much I hurt, humiliated, and surprised her by staying on the phone that Sunday after New Year's and finding out that I was still in love with Claudia. I thought it was obvious, but you can't argue with a woman who has tears in her eyes and a 27-inch Mitsubishi in her arms, so I gave her the letter and took the TV. (Years later, the friendship returned, even if Asia, Claudia, and Yvette didn't.)

The next few weeks and months Asia and Claudia would call and say how much they loved me; and I would tell them both the same thing.

Asia and I would often have phone sex. Once, while driving on I-45, she told me that the Secret Service jams cell phone service around George Bush Sr.'s residence, so if I was going to make her come, I had better hurry.

A few weeks after seeing her in Houston, Asia met me in a blonde wig and a short black dress at the Jacksonville airport. I was working the Comedy Zone at the Ramada Inn. She was holding a dozen roses as I got off the plane; I bought her a silver bracelet, but only because I couldn't figure out how to travel halfway across the country with a meatball sandwich.

It had been six years since that lunch in Tucson when I gave her the Joan Didion book.

"Did you ever think," I asked as I pulled at her hair, "you and I would be here?"

"You want to fuck me with the wig on?"

"Is that a line from *Slouching Towards Bethlehem*?"

"Let me tell you the joke—The ant and elephant joke." She told it slowly, and when she got to the *It was beautiful* part, she took a pause, smiled, and said, "How did I do?"

"Perfect."

She could only stay three days and had to bring her cell phone, so the flight instructor, who thought she was in northern Florida doing a *Versace* ad, could get hold of her. I used to leave the hotel room when he called, ostensibly to give her privacy, but also to go down to the hotel lobby to check my messages in Tulsa to see if Claudia called.

Asia and I went to St. Augustine one afternoon, and I took pictures of her sitting on car hoods, in front of restaurants, at the entrance to an old castle, and, my favorite, straddling a 17$^{th}$ century cannon, sucking on a lollipop, in an unbuttoned blouse.

One night Lenny Schultz, who was headlining that week came over to Asia and me. Lenny frenetically worked with a stage full of props, music, and X-rated puppets. Part of his act was having three or four Alka-Seltzer tablets dissolve in his mouth while the foam dribbled down his chin.

Still a mess from his show, he said to Asia, "You're beautiful, you know that?" Lenny asked her in front of me.

"We know, Lenny," I said.

He continued. "I've been doing comedy 30 years; I'm sixty-two. I don't look it, do I? I still got it, though, don't I?"

Asia smiled and kicked me under the table.

Later that night, in bed, Asia asked if all comics were weird.

"No, don't be ridiculous. Now put the wig back on."

I'd watch as she put on jeans over her very long legs; I'd walk into the bathroom while she was in the shower just to see the outline of her body against the curtain; I'd watch her read a newspaper, laugh at something on television, eat a candy bar, and smile at a baby at the mall. Asia was like one of those dreams that you know is a dream. It's too perfect to be real. And no matter how hard you try to stay asleep and prolong it, you know you're going to wake up soon.

On our last night in Jacksonville, we went to Albertson's and bought a two-liter Coke and a package of peach Pull N Peel licorice. As we sat on the bed and devoured the bag and drank from the bottle, I thought I should tell her I loved her, thought I should tell her that I had never gotten over those lunches in Tucson, thought I should ask her to stay, but I didn't. There was Claudia, for one thing, and then there was her cell phone, for another, which began to ring.

The next day, at the airport, she stood in blue jeans, an over-sized white dress shirt, and work boots. It was impossible for this girl to not be beautiful.

"I can't look at you too long."

"Why?"

"'Cause I can't concentrate on what I'm trying to say. You ever get tired of people telling you you're beautiful?"

"Only when they're trying to get me in bed."

"*I'm* trying to get you in bed."

"You got me in bed the first time you told me that ant and elephant joke."

"Would have been nice if you told me."

"You were married; I was seventeen. It seemed like bad math."

"Why do I feel that if I asked you to move in with me right now, you would?" I asked.

"You'd be right."

"What about your boyfriend?"

"What about Claudia?"

She smiled, kissed me, grabbed the back of my neck, pulled me close, and then told me the ant and elephant joke . . . again. This was another of those moments that I wanted to get exactly right because I had a feeling I'd never hear her tell it again.

I was right.

#!!°?)*%#*!( • ?#

With Claudia, I could be sure she was in Hamburg, chain-smoking with her brother, or in Lubeck, teaching some classmate how to fuck, or even in Spain, trying to make nice with her parents, but Asia was different. She didn't leave forwarding numbers, addresses, or, as I would find out, friends or family who would tell you where she was.

Unfortunately, nobody I've ever loved disappeared any better than Asia.

And then, two weeks later, I went to the Bahamas to meet Claudia.

All right, so you can't go home again, but I was hoping you could at least go for a visit, which is why I stood by an over-priced juice machine in what passes for the airport on Paradise Island, waiting for her to get off the plane. There was something inevitable and impossible about being here, waiting for her, but that's part of the charm of the island: fantasies seem well within reach. The Bahamas give you hope long after you know better. Claudia's shirt stuck to her back, and my hand, as I hugged her in front of a fat customs' official. She was wearing a stupid Duke University baseball cap, which poked me in the forehead, as I kissed her. On the way to the hotel, the cab driver told us he was also a priest, so if we wanted to get married, he'd do the ceremony. If not, he'd be glad to take us back to the airport when we left the island.

During that week, Claudia would stare at the sand for hours, gently scraping her nails across her chest, eating Mentos, drinking coffee, reading magazines. She'd want to go scuba diving, she wouldn't want to leave the room; she'd want to go dancing till 5AM; she'd want to go to sleep at 8PM. She was a caged animal.

One afternoon, as we sat by the lagoon, watching the new Royal Towers being built across the inlet, she reached across the lounge chair to touch my hand. She didn't say anything; she didn't look at me. I stroked her fingers; I heard her exhale. Like so many moments down here, this one was in slow motion. What can I tell you? It's the Bahamas. Suntan lotion smells good, three-dollar Cokes (tip not included) are the norm, and losing your luggage seems insignificant. But then you notice that suntan lotion stains your shirts, the Diet Cokes keep you awake, and some things in your suitcase were irreplaceable.

At Joker's Wild that night, I watched Claudia watch me on stage and knew that I was loved—that is, until she went back to Hamburg, where she opened a dress shop and where, years later, she would get a tattoo and try to slit her wrists in a bathtub.

On the way to the airport—she left first—I knew we had been too self-consciously tender and passionate, and maybe we were working off an old script, but we were usually better when we knew our lines. And anyway, against this backdrop, 100 yards from the Atlantic, even near-perfection can bring you to tears. The Bahamas are relentless. And love loves a sunset—even if you never get to find out what it's like to be married by a cab driver.

When I got back home from the Bahamas, I spoke to Asia a few times, but soon her phone was disconnected and my letters came back with the stamp of a red finger advising me that no such person existed at that address. I thought I heard her one time on MSNBC's *Hardball with Chris Mathews* and I did find her on the Internet a few years later. I think she married the flight instructor.

I saw a picture of Asia a few years ago in an *US* Magazine story about modeling. She had gained weight, streaked her hair, and was wearing a strange silver and green outfit. As for Claudia, she sends an e-mail every so often, written in German, which reminds me that she still plays the game better than I do.

Asia once mentioned she had been to Hamburg to model and went into Petra Teufel, the clothing shop Claudia worked in during college and eventually bought.

"I do remember one very pretty, shy girl," Asia told me.

"What do you think you would have said to her had you known?"

"You ever tell her the ant and elephant joke?" she asked.

For the first half of 1996, I was the ant.

I keep a black portfolio case in my closet of Asia's cards and letters and panties and red scissors and St. Augustine photos; I have a box under my bed of German love poems, cassettes, and pictures of Claudia with Japanese tourists in Berlin.

Now if I could just stop feeling guilty about those olives.

## CHAPTER 15

# The box under the bed

n my nightmares, I always seem to be in Europe, so being in Spain in this particular installment, in Mallorca, and being chased through the narrow streets of Palma by six men in t-shirts and dress pants wasn't unusual. Nor was Claudia's presence in the dream, for she was always in the bad ones. What was odd was that my dead mother and Claudia's non-existent husband were with us, too. As the men got closer, my mother, the husband, and I ducked into a poor Catholic church, where we hid behind some pews, but Claudia, for reasons not entirely clear, continued running towards a piazza near the Mediterranean. She was vomiting into a fountain when I woke up.

I never found out what the men wanted, but I remember one asking my mother, who sat listless in the rectory, "Where is she?"

My dreams of Claudia would never be a refuge for me, I knew that, but there was something about this one, the choreography between the dead and the dangerous and the sick, that made me unusually anxious. Claudia and I hadn't seen each other since I made a horrendous trip to Germany in December of 1997, a year-and-a-half earlier. I was supposed to stay two weeks, but after three nights of arguments and silence, I found a way to explain to a German cab driver to take me to the airport.

*Hi Love*

*Was going to Spain, but doctor says I have ovarian cancer. Bad things inside me. Very rare for a 28-year-old, he said. Operation soon.*

*Claudia*

It was the first e-mail she had ever sent me. And I got it the morning after the dream.

"Do you want me to come?" I called to ask. I still had her number memorized.

"I'm afraid if you do; I'm afraid if you don't."

Death would change everything about us except the relationship.

I could imagine her dying, lying in a German hospital bed next to a folding table full of pain pills, cancer drugs, stool softeners, and half-drunk apple juice boxes with straws hanging out. I thought of her hair, which I used to joke had a concentration camp buzz-cut quality to it, scattered in clumps around her pillow. Her mouth and eyes would be open but look like they belonged on different faces. I thought of the tattoo on her shoulder that she now had but I hadn't seen—I would tell her I liked it. I imagined her teeth, already stained from too many Winstons, trying to smile. I could see myself feeding her Almond Joys and Mounds and sitting on the edge of her bed and reading her Joan Didion and John Irving as she tried to stay awake. I thought, at best, if she lived, she'd lose her ovaries; at worst, she'd be dead within six months. And if she lived, I'd marry her. I had Paul and Nina; I didn't have to have more children.

Even if she did survive, I knew the cancer would come back in five years to kill her. In the months leading up to her death, I could see myself pushing her, now my wife, around in a wheelchair and using a syringe to give her water when she could no longer swallow. In the week before my mother's death, I changed her depends and wiped her ass. I cleaned vomit from her mouth; I would do the same for Claudia. The day my mother died—it was on a Thursday night—I watched her stare at the ceiling as she stopped breathing; I wondered if Claudia would do the same. If she would, I'd help her look at the pattern of the paint strokes above her bed; then, I would gently lie down next to her and try to avoid the tubes, the smell, the brittle bones, the sore skin, and wait for her to die. I would hold her hand when it came, sing to her, stroke her face with my fingertips, kiss her forehead, rub an ice cube on her lips, and try to close her eyes when she finally succumbed.

I knew she would die like this, but I knew she might not want me to be around when she did, so I could see getting a phone call from her brother telling me about, if not actually inviting me to, the funeral. I'd fly to Hamburg on what would be a gray October day, get in one of the Mercedes taxis lined up at the airport, and try to find the cemetery. I would get angry with the minister for getting the facts of her life wrong and I'd look at the 20-something German males standing around Claudia's casket and wonder who, among them, had slept with her. I'd hug her parents, Gertrude and Guenther, and tell them how much I loved their daughter. I could see myself after the funeral, at Claudia's apartment, trying to find the letters she said she had written me but never sent. I'd steal a picture, a shirt, something that wouldn't be missed, and then go home and place what I had taken in the cardboard box I had under my bed. Someday, I knew Nina would ask about it, or Paul, or even some girl who, after spending the night, would come across it while looking for an earring or bracelet.

I went back to sleep and tried not to have another dream, but when I woke, I couldn't remember if I had or how long I had slept. I felt nauseated; my legs and back ached. When I saw myself in the mirror, I was crooked.

I crawled under the bed and pulled out a box—her box. Inside I found a photo album from Spain, a retrospective of the Bergen-Belsen concentration camp, a Lufthansa boarding pass, one sock, which read *You are a* (I had lost the other one, that one that read *Heartbreaker*), two of the thirty-seven roses, now long dead, she had laid on my pillow for my 37th birthday, a cassette of alternative European bands that she had put together, a picture of the two of us in the red Miata, an InterCityExpress train schedule, a European formatted VHS copy of *Casablanca*, which I couldn't play, assorted letters, faxes, and postcards of our five years, and a poster of a young German boy in hard shoes and a multi-colored beanie. The boy was standing behind a barbed-wire fence and looking up at an armed East German guard on the other side of the barrier. The picture was from Berlin in the sixties and was taken from behind the boy, so only the reaction of the soldier could be seen—and he was either smiling or sneering. Claudia had written me on the back in three different pens. She wrote poetry, drew pictures, included recipes. I was going to frame the poster, but I didn't know which side I wanted facing out.

She nearly died once before, and you'll have to trust me on how I know the details of this story. When she was in graduate school, she was living in an apartment in the northern German city of Lubeck. One Sunday night, she was chain smoking, listening to a German band called Dead Trousers, and feeling the same mix of chill and heat in her body that I used to tell her I experienced—only she felt both simultaneously. She called her brother, Ollie, asked him to come over for dinner, and then filled up the tub, got in, took out her plastic blue Bic razor, and made two small x's on the backs of her hands. She knew she should cut the inside of her wrists if she were serious, but looking at those veins, in the lukewarm water, she got scared. It would be painful. She didn't even know if what she did counted as a full-fledged suicide attempt; still, she sat in a half-filled tub, looking at the grout on the tile, the blood beginning to fill in the marks on her wrists, and waited to die. *What the hell am I supposed to be waiting for anyway . . . wisdom?* None came, and she was getting bored, so she started telling a joke to herself that I had once told her—the same snail joke I had told Asia.

She giggled thinking about that poor snail. *Giggling,* she thought, *why am I giggling?* She remembered me also telling her that if people were not laughing by the *three years later* line, you could stop telling it—the joke was not being understood. She wanted to call me and tell me she got the joke, always had, but she had no phone in the bathroom and wouldn't have known what to say if I asked why she was calling. *Nothing, I'm just having a hard time slitting my wrists. How are you?*

Besides, she was getting cold and didn't want to get out of the water. She also stopped bleeding by now and knew she wasn't going to die, so she just waited for her brother to arrive. She sat up in the tub and finished reading *A Prayer for Owen Meaney*, which was sitting on top of the toilet.

She called a week later, after she was let out of outpatient care at a local hospital, to tell me about Nik, her childhood psychiatrist she had slept with; told me about how, one night after sleeping with a waiter who bought her a warm meal, she took a walk through the Reeperbahn, a peculiarly twisted pornographic district of Hamburg, and got the tattoo of the gargoyle with a dagger on her left shoulder; told me about the other four men and one woman she slept with that year; told me about her dress shop, which she was expanding, and her trips to the fashion shows in Paris and Milan; told me about her brother's new wife, a girl she described as having "hair on her teeth"; and then told me about how not a day goes by that she doesn't think of me.

The suicide attempt was neither the first thing she told me nor the last.

"What was it that writer said that you liked?" she asked.

"Joan Didion?"

"Yes. What was it . . . something about running away to . . .?

". . . She said that sometimes you 'run away to find yourself and discover that's there's no one home.'"

"Yes, that one. You never told me what happens to the girl she's talking about—the one who runs away?" The voice hurries when it hurts.

"Well, it's Didion herself, I think. And she becomes the type of woman who wants to live in a house with a moat."

"*I* sometimes do." She was excited. "Maybe that's why I'm calling."

I invited her to Tulsa because I sometimes did too.

This is a game we played, and we both knew our parts. Being in love with Claudia was like getting punched in the stomach but never actually feeling the blow.

She didn't come, of course. She faxed me the night before she was to arrive to say she was going scuba diving in El Salvador instead. She had cancelled trips before at the last minute, so I was used to returning gifts to jewelry and clothing stores that I had waiting for her. But this time, I also found myself at Albertson's, trying to get a cashier to take back the coffee, the Winstons, and the frozen pizzas. One time, Claudia sent me a check for $2,000 to make up for some unrefunded airfare. I thought that showed a certain maturity and responsibility for someone so young. "Either that," Don said, "or her rich father said, 'You mean we can be rid of this Jew for two grand? Cut him a check.'" Anyway, the fax about going scuba diving was, until the e-mail about the cancer, the last time I had any contact with her.

I was reading the last paragraph from a letter she wrote (and actually sent) weeks before she got in the tub with her Bic razor . . .

*You taught me half of everything I know about life, and since that night in the Bahamas, my heart doesn't work the same. You've ruined me from ever being able to love again because everyone else is a bad copy of you. I never feel comfortable telling you that I love you because when I do, I realize I'm not even close to describing why.*

. . . when I felt my back spasm.

I stretched out on the floor, put my hands under my chin, and waited for my sciatic nerve to stop screaming. My head was under the bed and I noticed I needed a new box spring; then I saw a garment bag, an old pair of New Balance running shoes, an eight-month-old *Newsweek*, and feathers from my leaking down comforter. *Could I be any more pathetic?* Finally, my back eased its grip, so I crawled out and sat on the floor, leaned against the bed, and put everything but the poster back in the box. The metal bed frame felt good against my back. I noticed what a lousy job the painters had done where the wall met the ceiling.

Maybe she loved me too much; maybe not enough. It was possible she knew when she took that ice cube from my mouth at Columbus

Tavern that she might someday wind up dead and bloody in a bathtub with a wet John Irving paperback nearby. Maybe she knew how troubled she was. The worn-out pictures of family photo albums, the anguished, distant echoes of those haunted train stations, graves, phone calls, and the sound of her own voice were just part of it. Almost everything about her was about something else. Maybe, though, she was just out of her fucking mind. But anyway, she was dying. It wouldn't matter soon. She would be a good ghost.

CHAPTER 16

# Death and Comedy

ell, she didn't die. The cancerous shadow in her ovary turned out to be a splintered IUD in her uterus.

But someone else did.

It's a two-hour drive on the Garden State Parkway from Atlantic City to the Verrazano Bridge, another hour and a half on the Belt Parkway from Brooklyn to Pinelawn, New York, on the southern shore of Long Island. You ride past overflowing landfills, 24-hour diners, sneaky highway patrolmen hiding out in tall grass, hundreds of orange cones protecting road crews eating lunch, and what seems like $4,000 in tolls, collected every twenty feet—all of which ensures that the entire trip is miserable, and not just the part about arriving at New Montefiori Cemetery and your mother's grave for the second time.

The last time I saw it, three months earlier, she was being lowered into it, so the grooves of the Star of David engraved in her casket had just been filled in with dirt.

It was now time to get her a headstone, which was why my father, sister, and I were making this insufferable drive again.

My mother was buried, as my father will be, as I will, at New Montefiori, in a plot of land purchased by the Yankef-Leibisch Family in the early 1930s. The Yankefs and Leibisches were my father's relatives, and consisted of his mother's nine brothers and sisters and their assorted wives, husbands, and children. Buying burial plots was the first thing many of these families did when they came over from

Europe; forming family groups, or circles, was the second. It would be during these Sunday afternoon get-togethers that the Yankefs and Leibisches would sit around in a circle in folding chairs, discuss politics, rehash real and imagined slights, eat pastrami sandwiches, slurp borscht, play pinochle, and generally scream at each other. They would also lament the family's financial state, which was always dire and always said to be the fault of the relatives who were late on their dues. By the time my father and mother had children, in the fifties, much of the Yankefs and Leibisches had dispersed throughout the other four boroughs of Manhattan, to New Jersey, and even, God forbid, the suburbs of Long Island, so there was always plenty of bitching about how long it took to get to the meeting as well.

There's a wonderful scene in the movie *Avalon*, where the character played by Lou Jacobi complains about such a trip, and then storms out of the house when he discovers one of his brothers started the Thanksgiving meal before he arrived. "You cut the turkey? Without me, your older brother?" He asks his younger brother. And then, before getting in his car, Jacobi screams from the street, "When you wanted to come to this country, I said *okay*. When you wanted to open a business and needed money, I said *okay*. And this is how you show your respect? By cutting the turkey?" It's a funny, petty, and heart-wrenching scene and one my relatives had three, four times a year. Like many families, the Yankefs and Leibisches lost their hearing, eyesight, hair, sexual prowess, and ability to walk pretty, but never their memories. Often I'd hear someone at these meetings warn another, "I'm going to keep a record of this!"

The major benefit of belonging to our family circle, according to my mother, was that you got to be buried in this family plot—for free.

"That's it?" I asked. "That's all the family's got to offer?"

"What can I tell you, Ba," she said. "When you're pushing up daisies, you'll be near family."

"Hey, don't kid yourself," my father added. "Do you know what a burial space costs these days?" he asked, ever the accountant.

*My parents were married for 35 years. They split up for a year; then they got back together, but my father's an accountant, so when you ask him how long he's been married, he asks, "Gross or net?"*

She did tell me, however, that only Jews could be buried in the family plot—even if I married a woman who wasn't—something I eventually did.

"She'll just have to go somewhere else," my mother added.

"*Go* somewhere else? You mean I can't be buried next to my own wife?"

"Not in this family you can't."

It was all pretty silly back then, but after I discovered my mother had been paying my $18 per year family circle dues to ensure my plot for the past 25 years, I realized how important it was to her.

#!!°?)*%#*!( • ?#

"Where is she?" my father asked, and he walked over and between headstones. He wasn't asking spiritually; he simply couldn't find her. I couldn't either. We were, I thought, at the exact spot where my mother should be, but there was only a temporary marker with the name *Betty Koralcheck* on it.

"Barry?" Susan asked.

"I have no fucking idea."

My mother was nowhere to be found. She used to bitch in restaurants about where the hostess sat her, and, now in death, apparently got herself moved because she didn't like where she was placed either. We went back to the cemetery office where Corky, a 19-year old receptionist, said, "She's there." My father starts getting apoplectic when Corky asks if we'd like to wait for the foreman. Good idea. He comes out of the back office, pulls out the master plot list, and says, "She's there." My father now *is* apoplectic, at which point the foreman points to

Betty's grave and says it's my mother's.

"Listen, Ronsencrantz," I tell the foreman, "she's not there."

"Yes, she is," he insists, and then tells me that Betty Koralcheck was buried right next to my mother.

"You were standing on her when your mom was buried. There was dirt and a green tarp so you didn't notice."

All four of us then went back to the plot with the schematic and discovered my mother was indeed buried immediately to the right of Betty; unfortunately, a temporary marker had never been put up.

"Hey, Dad," I said, "can you imagine the grief Mom is giving Betty about being so close?"

"Well, she's close to *my* mother at least," he said.

"Oh, yeah, that'll cheer her up."

Strange thing about family circle plots: you see exactly where you're going to be buried and who you're going to be next to. My father found his parents' grave, his brother's, whose stone read, *Why make things easy when with a little bit of effort you can make them difficult*, and where he would be buried—right to my mother's left.

"I don't care what you have to do, but when the time comes, you get me back here, you understand," my dad said.

It was both sad and funny to think about coming here someday to see my mother and father . . . and Betty. I saw approximately where I would be buried, too, down the road and out of the shade.

You can only spend so much time looking at an unmarked plot of land, so before we left, according to Jewish custom, we each put a stone on her grave. My father put one on his mother's, father's, and brother's grave, as well, and I placed one on Betty's. (A year later, I took Nina to a Yahrzeit (memorial) service, on the anniversary of my mother's death, and as the Torah made its way around the sanctuary, Nina touched it with her prayer book and then, according to tradition, gently kissed the book. My mother would have liked that last part.)

We then went to the *stone place*, as my father kept calling it. He had heard of this one company, Strung Mortuary, which the family circle had used for years. In fact, the week leading up to our trip, he kept talking about Strung. "We have to go to Strung," over and over like he was doing an ad for the place. He would hear of no other place. Strung Mortuary was a few miles away from the cemetery, but on the drive there, I noticed a *stone place* right across the street, so I suggested we go there.

"But what about Strung?" my father asked indignantly.

"What, do you have stock in the company?"

"Barry," my sister said, I'm sure imagining a new five minutes in my act. "Cut it out."

"All right, all right," he said, "We'll try this place. I have to go to Strung? I'll go where I want to go. Nobody's going to tell me where I have to go."

I could hear my mother.

*Who told you that you had to go to Strung anyway?*

Shopping for headstones is like shopping for computers: there are too many choices and you have no idea what you really need. There were stones of black granite, gray, and something resembling a pink, which was called "desert rose." And, in a rare display of family unity, we agreed on the pink. We inscribed it with my mom's name, a small menorah, the dates of her birth and death, and the words *For Family*. She used to say, "Friends can be replaced, but family, well, for family, you do anything."

Besides, at $11.50 per letter for engraving, *For Family* was cheaper than *Beloved wife, mother, grandmother, and friend.* (When I called my brother in California, he asked why we didn't inscribe the words: *For the Family,* and I told him because "We're not Corleones; we're Friedmans. Mom never said [I was impersonating Brando] 'for the family'; she said [I was impersonating Shelly Winters] 'for family.'")

The stone picked out, the inscription agreed to, we were about to leave when the *stone place* saleswoman said something a bit ominous. "I'll just get approval from the family circle, and we'll get started."

"Why do you need approval from them?" I asked.

"It's their land," she said, "and they might have rules and regulations about what kind of stone, etc. I mean, I don't see there being a problem."

Well, she never met Ida Meltzer, president of the family circle.

When I got home, I first called Lenny Meltzer, Ida's brother and head of the Yankef and Leibisch Family Burial Committee (yes, incredibly, there is one) to tell him the news about my mother and the choice of stone.

"Did you go to Strung?"

"No."

"What color did you pick?"

"It's desert rose, Lenny."

"What's that?"

"Pink."

Silence.

"Well, I can't ok that," he said. "You must talk to Ida to get such a thing approved."

"Such a thing approved?" I repeated. I sensed a problem.

When I called Ida, she wasn't home, but Lou, her husband, whom everyone calls "Red" even though he's bald, said, "Tell me the problem." I do and he says, "I can't make a decision like that. You'll have to wait for Ida."

It's now 11.30PM. My father's asleep. The phone rings.

"Hello, this is Ida Meltzer."

"Ida. Barry Friedman. Jack and Florence's son."

"I'm sorry *fuh ya* loss, Barry. Now about the stone."

She goes on to tell me that we cannot have a pink stone because in the family circle by-laws it says that all stones must be uniform in height and width and color, even though, she adds, "There's nothing specific about the color. It is, however, an unwritten law."

I say, "Ida, if it's an unwritten law, it shouldn't be tough to break."

"I *implaw* you; I *implaw* you. It has to be a gray stone. Your mother's stone must be consistent with the other stones on the plot; otherwise, we could have one black, one pink, one gray, one God knows what. Now, if you want me to call a special meeting of the cemetery committee, I will, but I *implaw* you, do not order the pink stone. If you do, I will not approve. That is final."

"You're kidding me, right? How often do they meet?"

"I'd have to call a special session. Some are in Florida, some are in New York."

"You are actually telling me the family circle has to come together from all over the country to discuss the color of my mother's headstone?"

"Mr. Friedman, we have our laws."

"But they're unwritten ones apparently."

"I am READING THEM to you!" she screams. "I am telling YOU there is no mention of pink, but it cannot be done! I am the President!" I tell her I have to check with the family and then I'll get back to her. We hang up.

If my mother were alive, and the stone had been for my father, sister, or me, she would have said, "Ida, it's going to be pink. Do you understand me? If you don't like it, when you go to the cemetery, I suggest you don't look at it."

Anyway, the next day Lenny called my father and was all shaken up (apparently Ida called him after she called me) and he begged my father to get a gray stone; my father agreed. I told my father we should have called a special meeting of the Burial Committee, if for no other reason than to overthrow Ida and install our own people. He replied, "We'll all be dead before they manage to scratch themselves to have a meeting." Later my father told me, sweetly, "What are we fighting about? Your mother shouldn't even be there. She should have had another ten years;

it wouldn't have killed anybody."

The night my mother died, my brother and I were sitting on either side of her bed, which was both the best and worst place to be. My dad had fallen asleep downstairs, watching *ER*. We all knew she would die that day, so the previous night, my father went up to see her and had fallen asleep next to her, holding her hand. When the moment came the next day, though, I thought it best to get him upstairs before telling him, so I made up some story about her needing him. (To this day, he swears he was in the room when she died.) A hospice nurse was then called. She came over, confirmed her death, and flushed my mom's unused pain and cancer medicine down the toilet. The funeral home people then arrived to carry my mom's body downstairs to a waiting tan-colored van and to the mortuary. Afterwards, my brother, sister, and I took my father to a diner. My father loves diners. I thought it might cheer him up.

And like chicken soup, it didn't really help, but it didn't hurt.

Most of the funeral arrangements had already been made, so the next day, my brother made plans for his wife, Monica, to come in from California, and then helped my sister vacuum and shampoo the smell of death from the carpet in my parents' bedroom. I spent the day on the phone, finding a rabbi to perform the graveyard service, calling relatives, and doing stupid things like trying to cancel my mother's cell phone contract (Bell Atlantic wouldn't budge without a death certificate).

I also wrote my mother's oncologist and told him that, considering how we learned more about my mother's condition from the hospice nurse in 20 minutes than we had from him in two years, he had turned out to be quite a putz. A few months later, the letter was published in an on-line oncology magazine, but I never heard back from the doctor himself.

In the Jewish religion, a person is supposed to be buried within 24 hours of death, unless the date falls on the Sabbath, in which case the family is given a 24-hour extension. Since my mother died on a Thursday night, she couldn't be buried until Sunday. Jews, as a rule, don't believe in embalming; funeral homes, as a rule, do—especially if burial doesn't take place within 24 hours. Ed, my mom's brother, checked with his rabbi and was told that state law trumps religious law in a case like this, but, if it were at all possible, we should try not to have an embalming done.

It's a good thing you only have conversations like this a few times in your life.

Wayne relayed the embalming predicament conversation to his wife Monica, a Seventh Day Adventist, who said she had done some research on the Internet on Jewish burial practices and discovered that Jews have absolutely no opinion on embalming—proving that the fewer people involved in burial matters the better.

#!!°?)*%#*!( • ?#

My mother and Monica were not great friends. Wayne had been married before, and while it's a long story, my mother had a special affinity for his first wife. My mother's cancer returned around the time of Wayne and Monica's wedding, so she couldn't travel to California for the ceremony. I think Monica took it personally; by contrast, my mother felt Monica broke up my brother's first marriage.

They were both wrong.

A few months before he married Monica, Wayne told my mother that Monica was the most passionate woman he had ever known.

"Doesn't he know, Barry," my mother asked after Wayne left, "that as soon as they get married, she's going to close up shop?"

"Close up shop?"

"Yes," she said. "The legs are going to close together," she slapped her hands loudly with her elbows together, mimicking a pair of thighs closing, "and that's all—no more sex. She's finished. That's all!"

My mother had a quaint sense of humor.

When my sister got pregnant with her fourth child, my mother was visibly annoyed, feeling it was the last thing Susan, who had gained some weight with each previous pregnancy, needed. I tried to convince my mother that it was Susan and her husband's decision and, really, when you thought about it, it wasn't any of her business anyway.

"You know, Mom, in Texas," I said, "they have an expression: 'I ain't got no dog in that fight.' Well, mom, you have no dog in this fight."

My mother looked at me, looked at Susan, looked back at me, and said, "I have a dog," she laughed. "There's my dog." She pointed to Susan. "I have a big dog."

On Saturday, I made more calls, including one to Claudia, whom I hadn't spoken to in a year. When someone you love dies, you start thinking about all the other people you love. And even though she had never met either of my parents, Claudia sent my father this fax twenty minutes later:

> Although we don't know each other, I would like to send you this fax & tell you how sorry I am, how my thoughts are with you and your family. I love Barry so much that I instinctively began to love his family & friends as well. All the stories I heard about you were wonderful, so right now I feel the loss of a wonderful person I never met. I am sending you, Barry & the rest of your family all my strength & love. If there is anything I can do, please let me know. It'll get dark here pretty soon & I will light a candle for all of you—especially Flo.

"Very nice, Barry. Very sweet. What's the story with her, anyway?"

"Believe me, dad, not now."

Later, Claudia wrote me and said she wanted to take care of me. She was afraid, she said, that if she didn't, my mother, who was sitting on a white puffy cloud, "would send down thunderbolts to burn my ass."

In another sweet gesture from someone who had never met either one of my parents, Marie called from Cleveland, where she had moved a few years earlier, and then sent a bucket of bagels.

The next day, Monica flew from California to New Jersey, and her plane was hit by lighting . . . twice—once in the air and once on the ground.

> *My mom died a few months ago, and the only reason I tell you is that when her daughter-in-law—my sister-in-law Monica—who my mother hated, flew in for the funeral, her plane got hit by lighting . . . twice. I thought, Ma, cut it out. This is your son's wife. Be nice. I usually find that mothers-in-law like that joke a lot more than the daughters-in-law.*

Sunday morning, we all had to leave at 4:30AM to get to New Montefiori for the 10:30AM burial. Since my sister knew the woman who owned the funeral home, we got a waiver on the embalming, but only if we got my mom in the ground before noon. I had a rabbi over the phone the previous day, gave him some facts about my mother, and told him my sister, brother, and I would be giving the benedictions. I had heard enough horror stories about rabbis getting the names, events, and even pronunciations wrong at these burials to make sure he had as few responsibilities as possible. He was to meet us at the grave and get $350 to do the 20-minute service. Comedians should do so well.

There were eight of us in a limo, which was designed for six. Ed, Anita, Wayne, Monica, my sister, and I were in the back of the limo; my father was in the front with my brother-in-law, who was driving and who would leave my sister a year later for a woman who delivered pizzas. My sister's oldest daughter rode in the passenger seat of the hearse. My mother would not have been happy. *In the hearse you're letting her sit . . . Emily?* She would have asked. My mother had a habit of putting those things at the end of sentences . . . her nouns.

It was raining, it was humid, and the limo was cramped as we made our way up the Garden State. On days like these, my mother would get in a car, immediately fan herself, motion to the air conditioner controls, and say to my father, "Everything on high, Jack. I need air, Jack. I'm dying. Numbers, Jack, numbers," she'd say, referring to the thermostat control dial. "What do you got it on?" We laughed about that a lot on the drive up the turnpike

An hour into the trip, we stopped at a Burger King for something to drink. Monica, however, apparently hungry for breakfast, bought a sausage and egg biscuit. We are not the most religious of Jewish families, but even the Friedmans understand the religions and culinary inconsistency of a sausage biscuit on the way to a Jewish funeral.

My father asked, "What's that smell?"

Nobody had the heart to tell him.

"You do know, don't you, what *Wayne* means, don't you?" Monica asked after finishing breakfast.

Nobody did, least of all my father.

"The wagon-maker," she said confidently.

I could have lost a spleen

"A what!?" I asked

"The wagon maker," she said in earnest, "You didn't know that?"

It's absurd to think of my father walking into my mother's hospital room on the day Wayne was born and sitting on the edge of the bed and saying expectantly, "Flo, did you see our baby? He has the hands of a . . . wagon-maker." Anita, who can have trouble with her bladder when she's in the middle of a good laugh, nearly peed in her pants. My brother is a sweet, loveable, embarrassingly generous guy who likes to work out, run, and exercise regularly, but when you think wagon maker, when you think of a short little man, alone in his shop, cobbling together iron and rubber and whatever else makes a wagon, Wayne isn't who you think of; when you think of little children going to the wagon maker's home and asking "Can I make wagons someday?" and the wagon maker, wearing an apron and holding a mallet, and saying, "Ah, yes, but first you must learn," Wayne is not the guy who comes to mind.

"What does *Barry* mean?" I asked Monica.

"Perhaps, the wagon maker's brother?" Ed asked.

"I don't know why you're laughing. It's true," she said, "Wayne is the wagon maker."

Ed looked like he was ready to cough up blood.

Wagon maker references, son of wagon maker references, incompetent wagon maker scenarios filled the limo for the next two hours, but Monica had fallen asleep so she didn't hear most of them.

*Names are very important. Let's say you're pregnant and you want to have a son and you want this son to be a brain surgeon, don't name him "Gator." I think women understand this better than men, because* (and here I point to a woman in the front row) *you're not going to a gynecologist named "Cooter," are you? And ladies, I'm with you, because if I'm going in for a pap smear, I'm not going to some guy wearing a* John Deere *cap.*

We arrived at the cemetery. It began to rain: a hard, angry, April rain. I hadn't felt a downpour like this since that lost year in North Hollywood. I thought about what that hospice nurse told me a few days before my mother died: that many times the person who is sick is afraid to die because he or she is afraid of leaving her family alone. The nurse said that it's good for family members to tell the person dying that it's okay to let go, that, before the sick can feel peace, they have to be assured that the family will look after each other. It's a sweet sentiment, and I whispered that in my mother's ear two mornings before she died.

Had she been able to talk, had she been able to understand, I'm sure she would have said, "Don't give me that crap."

"Ma, listen," I told her a day before she died, "you don't want to die, don't."

Feeling the pellet-like hits of the rain against my face and hands made me sure that she was giving somebody hell.

As Jewish families dispersed through America, they often lost ties to their temples and synagogues, and so when many of these Jews died, they found themselves in cities without a relationship to a rabbi. My parents were in that situation, which is why I was forced to call an unknown rabbi and ask him to perform the ceremony. As I said, rabbis make a good living doing these services. You can spot them walking around Jewish ceremonies, looking for grieving families in need. I can't remember the rabbi's name I hired, but he looked like a rabbi is supposed to: short, slight of build, bearded, and disheveled.

There were maybe 14 of us, standing around a mound of dirt and my mother's casket. There should have been more people there, and had my mother been alive, she would have kept a record of those who didn't show. Jews don't have open caskets, nor do they have viewings, but the day after she died, my father wanted to see her, so we went to the funeral home to view the body. The woman in the casket bore some resemblance to my mother, but not much. Standing at the cemetery a few days later, I felt like I was burying three women: the one who made me laugh at the way she tortured lazy waitresses, the one with the scared and hollow eyes who died not knowing her sons were holding her hand, and the one in the ankle-length dress and soft make-up lying in the casket.

The rabbi began the ceremony, and then, inexplicably, asked all assembled to recite their Hebrew names. Some didn't know theirs, some didn't have them, some were too shy or sad to speak, and some, namely two, didn't know what the hell he was talking about. Inadvertently, the rabbi had asked the gravediggers for their Hebrew names. "Huh?" one asked, leaning against his shovel. "What name is he talking about?" the other one asked. Like a good comic, the rabbi moved on to another bit, which was sure to work. He said some prayers in Hebrew and mentioned my mother's five grandchildren; unfortunately, she had seven. He had left out any mention of my children.

"Rabbi," I interrupted, "you forgot Paul and Nina."

"Excuse me," he said. He looked annoyed. And why not? I was heckling.

"You forgot two of her grandchildren, Paul and Nina."

"Oh, sorry."

He started again, inserting the right number before the grandchildren. My sister later told me that when my grandmother died, sixteen months before her daughter, that rabbi had forgotten to mention Paul and Nina as well, and my mother interrupted that service to correct that rabbi.

My brother then spoke about how our mother had taught him the importance of family, and how with the help of Monica, he was going to continue to love and cherish every moment of his life; Susan then reminisced about my mother's mismatched socks and house coats and how she would miss the sound of her voice; and then I spoke about how her death was the not the most important day in her life, or ours, and how she'd be really annoyed that Emily, her oldest granddaughter, was standing in the rain. I thought about the time I told my mom that Jane and I were getting divorced. "Look, Ba," she said, "you'll be fine, Jane will be fine, and the kids will be fine. Remember, nobody died."

My father, Susan, Wayne and I then sprinkled some dirt on the casket, said goodbye to the few relatives who had come, and then headed back down the Garden State to a home whose every inch would remind us of the woman who would eventually be lying in front of a gray headstone and too damn close to Betty Koralchek.

But first we stopped at a diner.

A few weeks later, my mother's oncologist suffered a massive coronary, which didn't kill him, but made his life unbearable for about 18 months.

*Ma. Cut it out.*

CHAPTER 17

# Help me off with my pants

hy was there such a fuss over *Angela's Ashes?* Once you get past the fried bread, weak tea, and wet clothes, there's not much there—certainly not much of a story. But in thinking about my life in comedy—the early morning wake-up calls in hotels, the schlepping of luggage through terminals looking for connecting flights, the finding of pieces of papers in pants pockets with phone numbers of women I couldn't remember, I realized there wasn't much progression in my narrative either.

But if one can glean perspective from the cold rain of an Irish morning, one can do the same from the stale, dead air of a Vegas casino.

Repetition defines you.

When I lived in North Hollywood, there was a club in Van Nuys called the Comedy Cabaret, where comics could more easily get stage time than at the Improv or Comedy Store. The Cabaret wasn't an "A" room; it was a dark, dank place in a strip center and few agents or producers ever went there to scout talent. Still, to get a showcase, a comic had to call the first Thursday of every month, between 10AM and 3PM, at which time the booker, and I forget his name, would schedule an audition. The booker would simply not do this at any other time during the month; hence, if you didn't talk to him on the designated Thursday, you'd have to wait another 30 days for a chance to audition at this club where, even if you were passed and given regular spots, nobody would see you anyway. For six months, on the designated Thursday, I called at

9:58AM, and put the automatic redial on, so the calls would be made every ten seconds or so until someone picked up. And for this one day every six months I sat, looking at the phone, hearing a busy signal on the speakerphone. Invariably, at 3:01 every Thursday afternoon, someone would pick up the phone and tell me the booker had just left and if I wanted an audition slot, I knew the rules, I had to call back the following month.

Another time, years later, I was trying to get work on a cruise ship, and my friend, a comedian, John Joseph, told me to call his agent about the booking. (John was once in the Bahamas with Claudia and me and commented that he had never met any woman who loved any man more than she loved me, but added, "The Barry I know isn't cut out for a girl like this.") John assured me that getting work on the cruise was all set; he had already put in a good word. I wouldn't have to send a tape; I just needed to call his agent and tell him when and where I wanted to work. I called the agent every week for a few months. He came to the phone once to tell me to call back.

I did. But he didn't.

And then this: Catch a Rising Star has a club at the Hyatt in Princeton, New Jersey. I started there as an opening act, and through the years, worked my way up to headliner. When I first started, Catch put up all the comedians at the Hyatt. As the years went on, the comics were moved to the less impressive Holiday Inn; then just the headliner was put up at the Holiday Inn; at last report, no comic was getting a room, which meant that unless you lived in the area, you couldn't afford to do it. And even if you did, standing at Princeton Junction station at 1AM, waiting for the last train back to Manhattan or Philly is not unlike the feeling a comedian gets driving an interstate in North Dakota. Catch in Princeton was one of the few rooms, outside of Vegas, which scheduled three shows on Saturday night: 7:00, 9:30, and 11:45. It was the only night of the week in the only club in the country that I actually felt like I worked for a living. I told my father once that on these

Saturday nights if you counted from the time I took a shower, say, around 5PM, to the time I went to bed, say 3AM, it was a ten-hour day, which, I surmised, compared with a real job.

"So, you see?" I chided. "I work."

"But nobody counts their work day from the shower. What kind of business is this that you're in? There are no loyalties, no future, no life. You run amok. No wonder you drive girls crazy. There's no life with you."

"*I* drive *women* crazy? And what's your problem, anyway? How much money do I have to make before you consider this a career?"

"A hundred and fifty-five thousand dollars."

"You *have* a figure? It was a rhetorical question."

One Saturday in Princeton after the 7PM show, the bartender called me over said there were people from *The Late Show with David Letterman* at the bar asking about me. He directed me towards the bar and to these two women in their mid twenties, who were both drinking beer and smoking.

"Hi," I said. "You wanted to see me?"

"Yes," the thin one said, "I'm (and I can't remember her name but I think it was Christine or Christina), and I work for the *The Late Show with David Letterman*, and I thought you were very funny."

"You know there are two things a comic wants to hear after a show," I said, "the first is 'I work for *The Late Show with David Letterman* and I thought you were very funny,' and the second is having some 19-year-old hard-body with long legs and perfect white teeth say, 'You were really funny. Say, would you help me off with my pants?' Of course, if the women from *Letterman* would ask me to help them off with their pants, well, *that* would be extra special."

"Well, how about if I just tell you the first?"

"That'll be fine."

"Would it be all right with you," she asked, "if we stayed for the next two shows? We really think you'd be perfect for Dave." I could see a scar down the middle of her chest. It looked like she'd had some kind of heart surgery, and I was hoping she wouldn't die before she got to tell Letterman about me.

"Would it be all right? Absolutely not. Now take your friend and get the hell out of here!"

They laughed, the bartender laughed, and I thought to myself that if I didn't fuck up the next two shows, I was going to be on *Letterman.* By the time I went on stage for the second set, I knew what I would wear on the show if I got it (black suit, white t-shirt), what material I'd use (mostly about being Jewish and living in Oklahoma), where I would eat after the show (Carnegie Deli), and at what hotel I'd stay (The New York Hilton). As I walked around the Carnegie Center in Princeton between the second and third shows, trying to calm down, I realized I had never been this close in comedy to an opportunity this good.

True to their word, the girls stayed. I did different material to show them variety, I worked the crowd to show them spontaneity, and I even changed clothes to show them different looks.

After the third show (I consciously stayed away from them during the first two so I wouldn't appear too anxious), I walked over to the girls who were still drinking and smoking. I noticed one of them had taken notes. This was encouraging.

"Different material; pretty impressive. You're very commanding and personable on stage. You look terrific. You obviously know how to dress," the girl with the scar said. Apparently the other girl was just a friend.

"So what happens now?" I asked.

"The show's on hiatus for a few weeks, but when everybody gets back, we'll have a meeting to discuss new talent. Now, understand, I don't book the show, but I will give Dave my highest review of your show."

*I will give Dave my highest review of your show.*

"Can I call you?" I asked. "I mean I know there's a fine line between being persistent and being a pain in the ass, and I promise to keep on the right side of the line, but can I call you?"

"Look, we're not allowed to give out phone numbers, but, believe me, you'll be hearing from us."

Okay, she was a little drunk, she didn't give me a card, she came with a friend who helped her pay the tab, and she did ask, "What are you doing later?" which sounded more personal than professional, but why would she have stayed for three shows? Why the notes? Why the wardrobe review?

In comedy, the criteria for success kept changing. When I first started out, I wanted stage time. When I got stage time, I wanted to be paid. When I got paid, I wanted to get paid enough to make a living. When I was on the road and getting paid enough to make a living, I wanted to work better gigs. When I worked the better gigs, I wanted to work Las Vegas. When I worked Las Vegas, I wanted to do television. When I did television, I wanted to do better television. And for me, *Letterman* was television.

If I could appear on *Letterman*, even if nothing else came of my career, I would feel validated . . . vindicated. The comedy car, the lack of a 401K plan, the looks from Jane and my dad and my kids, and the lonely walks in the malls on Saturday afternoons—all of it would be worth it. I could hear my dad at the craps tables in Atlantic City asking the croupier if he had seen me on *Letterman*; I could hear Jane's friends asking her the same thing. I could imagine Paul and Nina sitting cross-legged on the floor watching the show. I would remind them to set the VCR.

The next day I was in New York City and walked by the Ed Sullivan Theatre where *The Late Show* is filmed. I asked the guard by the office entrance whether there was a girl by the name of Christine or Christina who worked for the show. He said he wasn't sure, but if the girl I was talking about was painfully thin, then, yes, she did work there. He said he had heard something about the staff being on vacation and that some of them were scouting talent in different parts of the country. I felt even more confident. I walked down the street to Caroline's, a comedy club on Broadway, to set up a showcase. I felt more like a comedian than I had in years. I called comics I knew who did *The Late Show* to find out if my experience was normal, and was told it was. One comic, a good friend, Kenny Rogerson, said he actually auditioned for the show over the phone. (Kenny and I spent a lot of time together in the summer of 1999, at Catch at the MGM, playing nickel keno and walking around like old Jews in shorts looking for buffets. "I vant," Kenny used to say in a great Yiddish accent, "a nice piece of fish.")

I then spoke to a comic, Eddie Brill, who worked as the *The Late Show* house MC, and he said it was possible my name would be forwarded to the people who actually made the decisions, but not to count on it.

#!!°?)*%#*!( • ?#

In the weeks that followed, I told too many people about it, got Paul and Nina excited, and even Jane called and said, "So, I heard you're going to be on *Letterman*. Let us know. I'm sure the kids will want to watch."

Eddie was right, though. I shouldn't have counted on it. Nobody from *The Late Show* ever called. Maybe Christina's heart gave out just as she was walking into Letterman's office with my name on a piece of paper.

When I did *Stand Up, Stand Up*, a comedy show on Comedy Central, I received a call from someone at HBO who had seen my set. He was impressed, he said, and told me to overnight him my tapes, resume, and pictures. HBO was looking for a host of some show they were planning. He actually asked if I would be willing to leave Oklahoma. I also remember this call coming on the same day I was going for a job interview writing advertising—something I was doing when Jane first saw that message board about a comedy contest years ago. I was more broke than after I dropped off the tape, resume, and pictures at Fed Ex, I went to the job interview. In the span of twenty minutes I applied for a job I would love and I applied for one I'd hate.

I was offered neither.

Getting to do *Letterman* or to host a show on HBO wouldn't have made me any funnier; it just would have made me think I was. Most of the time, in comedy, the only voice I heard regarding my talent was my own—and it was a voice I couldn't always trust.

On Tuesdays, when I wasn't working the road, I'd go to Open Mike Nights at the Tulsa Comedy Club, which was the third club that had opened in Tulsa—the first two having succumbed to either greedy management, poor or non-existent advertising, or some combination of both. When I started out, I hated the ease with which working comedians would stroll into these clubs on these nights. While I would be pacing in the back of the showroom and going over my notes, these working comics would be flirting with waitresses and getting corporate gigs. If these comics performed at all on these nights, they acted as if they were doing the club a favor by gracing its stage on an Open Mike night. For us amateurs, though, it was the only night of the week we would actually be comedians, which is one of the problems with the business. Anybody can wake up any morning, do an open mike night that evening, and call himself a comedian the next day. The same can't be said for those wanting to be gynecologists; hell, the same can't be said for those wanting to be toll takers. On these Tuesday nights in the late '90s, I was now the comedian who strolled in late; I was now the comedian looked at with a certain mix of envy and anger (for taking a slot); and I was now the comedian who slept with local waitresses and got interviewed by local news stations. I was finally the comic I used to hate.

I wasn't writing as much new material, but the stuff I was, had more meat on it.

*I was at a club last Easter and someone yelled from the back booth, "You Jews killed our Lord." Hey, look, we didn't do it. And even if we did, he came back, so, in my book, no foul.*

*I hated* Titanic. *At the end of the movie, when she's lying on that piece of wood, it would have killed her to scoot over so he could have hopped on. What a selfish bitch! He saved your fat ass! Move the fuck over!*

*My ex-girlfriend taught me the difference between an issue and a problem. For instance, her house burned down—that was a problem. I guess why I set the fire would be the issue.*

The uncertainty of how a joke will be received is part of the excitement of being on stage. The more I did comedy, the better my instincts were on how a joke would be received. For instance, the *Titanic* joke I knew would work. Enough people hated the film, for one, but just as important, The *move the fuck over* line is just a funny sounding sentence. As for the *Christ* joke, I figured it would be hit or miss, and it usually was. Audiences don't always want to discuss those responsible for Christ's death. As for the *issue/problem* joke, only hardcore feminists dislike it, but you know what they say about a feminist's sense of humor. Right. They don't say anything about it, because feminists don't have any. (See? Now the response to that joke would illicit too many groans for me to do it on stage.) Videotaping one's show can help the comic remember the passion and detail (and sometimes even how it goes), but whenever I videotaped one of my shows, I wanted to throw it, and the VCR that recorded it, out the window.

I had my regular clubs—Catch in Vegas, Reno, and Princeton, The Maxim, The Riviera, Don's club in Houston, the Tulsa club (where, if you can believe it, Jane started working as marketing director), the Bahamas, and a few others. I did some corporate gigs and Christmas parties, as well as commercials for pizza places, car dealerships, and banks in Tulsa. I wasn't a big fish in a small pond; I was a medium-sized fish in a small pond.

There was a year a few years after my divorce that I lived at the Doubletree Hotel in Tulsa. I made a deal with the catering manager that if I performed in their lounge once a month, for free, I would be allowed to stay in the hotel, for free, when I wasn't on the road. The kids loved this arrangement, as the front desk personnel liked them enough to give them free tins of cookies when they came over. When they did, we'd go up to the VIP lounge on the ninth floor. There, the kids could drink Pepsis for free, eat fried appetizers, make phone calls, and see the skyline of Tulsa. Later we'd swim in both the outdoor and indoor pool and sit and look at the woods outside the hotel, which they thought of as their back yard.

Then, after the hotel got tired of the deal and Claudia cancelled one of my trips to Germany, I found myself with nowhere to go. Ed and Anita, who fortunately find me reasonably funny at times, invited me to stay with them. Their daughter, Katie, was at college, so I stayed in her room until I saved enough money to get a place of my own. It was fun standing in the kitchen at night and making Anita laugh as she made veal parmesan, but I once again found myself in someone else's home, staring at someone else's ceiling.

Much of the time in comedy, I felt like there was a studio audience following me around. In my mind, I would periodically check with them to see how things were going. Comedy, by design, is parasitic. The best jokes, unfortunately, are retold stories of broken promises, shared intimacies, infidelities, and others' embarrassment. In retelling them—either on stage or here—you're betraying a confidence of the people who mean, or once meant, something to you. I remember a line from *Absence of Malice* when Sally Field's boss, an editor, says to her, "I know how to tell the truth, I know how not to hurt people. I just don't know how to do both at the same time." Not that the comedy is truth, but it is evidence of truth (at least if it's done right). There are people I met who wanted to be included in the act (and then here in these pages); there are people who threatened to sue. And then there were people who came up to me after a show and told some filthy racist joke that had no punch line, no point, or, worse, no ending. They always felt like they were helping the act.

Once Jane and Bob came to my show in Tulsa and sat in the front row.

*My girl friend just broke up with me, and it's really tough to talk about. Well, because, I'm married. No, no, I'm divorced.* (At this point, I'll ask if any woman in the audience has ever been divorced, and when one raises her hand, I'll find out why she's divorced—usually because the husband cheated or was a drunk—and then say) *The women know what you're talking about; the men are thinking, 'Yeah, so, what else did he do?' I know why my marriage ended. I mean, I think. My ex-wife was an actress and she once did a movie with Anson Williams. Believe me, folks, you don't know what jealousy is until you think your wife's sleeping with Potsie.*

I then closed the show:

*A week after my divorce, a week!, my ex-wife married a 47-year old bald insurance agent named Bob. Coincidentally, about a month later, I started dating a 19-year-old German model, and my ex-wife said, "What do you have to say for yourself?" I don't know. I win. But that's not what I wanted to tell you. Anyway, because I travel, my son and I don't see each other that much, so we play this little game with each other when I come back. I'll ask him who the best daddy is in the world and he'll point to me, and then he'll ask me who the best son is in the world and I'll point to him. It's cute. Sure, it's nauseating, but cute. Anyway, one day we're playing this game and he says, "You're the best daddy in the world, but I also have the best step-dad and it's Bob." And now I don't want to play, so I say, "Look, he's not really*

*your step-dad.' And he says, 'Well, yeah he is, because Mommy mar-*
*ried him, he lives in the house, she loves him, she doesn't love you. That*
*makes him my step-dad, right?" I said, "No, it doesn't. It only makes*
*him your step-dad if you don't have a dad, and you have a dad. You*
*don't need a step-dad, you don't need anyone, so just remember some-*
*thing, as long as I'm alive, Bob is just a guy your mom's (long pause)*
*fucking." So we put him on Prozac and he should be better in three or*
*four years.*

Everything about that story is true—I did have that conversation
with Paul—except the line about *just a guy your mom's fucking.* And Bob,
as I've mentioned, did move in less than a week later. They got married
within the month. Asia actually gave me the line about the 19-year-old
model. When I first wrote the joke, I had the model being 22. "Twenty-
two is really too old for a model and, besides, the audience will think
you're a stud if you're bagging a 19-year-old," she said.

After that particular show, as the audience was filing out, Jane
turned, saw me coming towards the door that let out to the bar, and
said, "You need to get laid." Maybe I did; maybe I didn't.

"Don't worry," I said, "I'm doing fine."

For the record, Jane was the costume designer on the movie *All-
American Murder*, Anson's directorial debut, starring Christopher
Walken and Joanna Cassidy.

The joke about her having an affair with Williams was just that—a
joke. I visited Jane on the set once, and watching her kibbutz with
Williams, I thought how odd it would be if the two of them got together. How pathetic, how sad, and how much I would deserve it, if I lost my
wife to a guy who once played the part of a guy named Potsie. I mean,
Fonzie, okay, but not Potsie.

Funny thing was, years later at the Riviera, a comic heard me do that
joke about Jane and Anson, and asked if it was true. I told him probably not, but I guess it was possible. He then told me a story about his

wife and Anson back in the '70s, when she was working on the set of *Happy Days*. Now, according to the comic, this was when Anson was at his most popular and could have any woman he wanted. Anson was so afraid of getting girls pregnant, though, he wouldn't fuck them, but he would have oral sex.

"It's possible," he told me, "my wife blew Potsie. Wouldn't it be something if your ex did the same?"

Sure would.

Anyway, the morning after she and Bob came to the show, Jane called to say she couldn't understand why my act had gotten so nasty, that she had a reputation in this community, and as much as she hated the joke about her and Bob, it was the one about Anson that bothered her more. She said that if I continued doing it, she would sue me. I think I said something about that being okay, as I could use the publicity.

*My ex-wife came to the show last night and was so unhappy with that joke about her having an affair with Potsie, that she said she was going to sue me for slander. She actually went to an attorney, who looked at her and asked, "You fucked Potsie!? Wow, that's so cool." Anyway, she hates that joke even more than the other one now.*

All right, the whole episode is childish, vindictive, and unfair, but I was fairly certain that no other comic had a wife who may have had an opportunity to sleep with Potsie. And that was the point (if you didn't count my desire to annoy Jane), the joke was unique, and maybe by extension, my comedy might be viewed the same way.

As much as I enjoyed the years in comedy, the lazy afternoons of walking the Strip in Las Vegas with nothing to do but kill time until the evening shows, the anticipation of the women and the work, the adrenaline rush of complete strangers laughing at something I had created and girls with big smiles and good skin waiting for me after a show, I was always ambivalent about being a comedian. Comedy, even at its best, is like sitting at the kid's table during Thanksgiving. A comic once told me how he was playing a comedy club in Augusta, Georgia, home of The Masters Tournament. He was an avid golfer and, as luck would have it, he started fucking a waitress whose grandfather happened to be on the board of directors at Augusta National Golf Club. When the comic told the girl how much he wanted to play Augusta, she invited him over to her house to meet *grandpa*. So he goes to the house on Sunday morning, shakes hands with the grandfather, and introduces himself. Before he can say much, the grandfather says, "Oh, yes, you're the clown, right?"

"Well, I'm a comedian," the comic says, taken aback.

"As I said, you're the clown, right?"

The comic didn't even ask about playing golf, figuring *grandpa* wasn't going to let a clown anywhere near the venerable course.

I remember once in Vegas, Steve and I were talking about comedy and women and work and he said, "Look, Barry, you're a friend of mine, but I mean, you're not going to be the next Leno or Seinfeld. Enjoy yourself. Make a few bucks, fuck a few broads . . . it could be worse. What, you gonna complain?"

He was right. Not about the broads or the work or even the money. It was the other thing: the Seinfeld and Leno business. I wasn't going to take their place. By this time, we were sitting in his red Jeep Cherokee on Tropicana, between Arville and Wynn, when it hit me: I might be a comedian for years to come, might even get a couple of television spots, might even make some decent money at it some day, but I was not going to have my own television show or be the kind of comedian who became part of the national consciousness. I was just another comic. Period. I was not going to be on *Fresh Air* with Terry Gross talking about comedy, nor was I going to do an hour with Charlie Rose, nor be a panelist on *Politically Incorrect*. It wasn't that I didn't think I was funny—I did—but sometimes you just know when your talent, timing and luck are not enough. Even if Andy Warhol was right about everybody getting fifteen minutes of fame; he never promised they'd be on *Letterman*.

When I was 31, my brother asked me if I still wanted to be a comedian, working bars and Vegas, at 40.

"If I'm still enjoying it," I told him.

He reminded me of that conversation on my 43rd birthday.

For me, the best part about being a comedian was often just being able to call myself one.

## CHAPTER 18

# Amonymously yours

fter working with Gilbert Godfried at the Silver Legacy in Reno, Nevada, on New Year's Eve 2000, I came back to Tulsa and began dating a married Columbian girl with a very understanding husband; I saw Amonymous again; I met a girl in the Bahamas whose 16-year old brother was in prison for murder; I had a brief affair with a woman who was addicted at one point or another to alcohol, drugs, and sex (not to mention having a mother who appeared to be living in a Eugene O'Neill play and a father who had some issues with the holocaust—specifically that it never happened). I finished writing this book and then began gutting it of all signs of vitality and life; and I hit my son with an open hand.

But I didn't do much comedy, which may explain why I also started reading essays on a local NPR station and working part-time at the Tulsa Performing Arts Center.

My grandmother, a year before she died, told my brother she had everything she needed: family, reasonably good health, a comfortable place to live. She was, she said, happy, but still yearned for something more. Wayne figured youth, her husband back, some philosophical answer to why, how she arrived at a point in her life when home was a room in a nursing facility within walking distance of Bally's Grand and the Atlantic Ocean, but it was nothing like that.

"Cash. I have no dough," she said.

As good a name for a book about comedy as any.

In November of '99, The MGM threw Catch a Rising Star out of its showroom and replaced it with a live *Wheel of Fortune* game. (A few months later, they threw out the game, and put in Rita Rudner's one-woman show.) The Maxim closed that month as well, but not entirely. The gaming tables, two bar's slot machines, Comedy Max and Davinci's Restaurant were shut down, but the coffee shop and hotel stayed open—though it's tough to understand why anyone but a comic would want to stay in rooms 335, 337, or 339. Walking into the hotel one day a few months after it closed, I found it dark, cold, and barren—not all that different form when it was open. The posters of the comedians on the walls around Comedy Max were still there, but the placard announcing the present week's comedians was ripped out, leaving a broken plastic sheath inside a frame. The bar at the Cloud Nine Lounge was still standing, but littered with trash and dust and electrical wiring and plastic convenience store cups.

For all the weeks I worked Vegas in the '90s, I didn't work there at all in 2000. Steve and I weren't talking, so there was no work at the Riviera. As for the other hotels that still had comedy clubs, I had worked so much at the Maxim, Riv, and MGM that I had never bothered to get in with them.

Don got me a job on a gambling ship out of Corpus Christi, but cautioned me about the booking agent.

"You know, this is Steve's gig. I'm just making the call."

"Does this mean he and I are talking?" I asked.

"Well, through me you are, but I wouldn't be expecting a Christmas card."

#!!°?)*%#*!( • ?#

In March, I worked the Bahamas for three weeks with a guy who had his own sitcom on cable. One night, after the show at Joker's Wild, I was sitting at Dragon's Bar in the casino with three girls from Baltimore. One of them announced pretty proudly that she was a virgin, but had an inordinate crush on the famous comic. Soon, she disappeared, and when I asked where she had gone, one of her friends made a sucking motion with her hand and mouth to signify the girl was giving the guy a blowjob.

"I thought she was a virgin?" I asked.

"She is, but it's just a blowjob. And, anyway, the guy has a sitcom. Besides, she's not going to fuck him. She's got standards."

"Hey, I was in *UHF*. Does that get me a handjob?"


On this trip I also met Katrina, who was half German, half Asian. It reminded me of the joke about a new German/Chinese restaurant opening up. The only problem is, an hour after you eat there, you're hungry for power.

Katrina lived in Philadelphia, so the next time I was in Atlantic City visiting my dad, I met her for lunch on the boardwalk. Over stale breadsticks at Resorts, she said she was surprised that I kept writing to her.

"The only other guy who writes me so much is in jail. I met him when I went to visit my brother."

"Why's your brother in prison?" I asked. I'm thinking burglary, drugs, robbery.

"Murder."

Of course.

Apparently, when her brother was 14, he was doing drugs, and needed money, which, apparently, his 12-year-old girlfriend refused to give him—that is, until he stabbed her 97 times. I may have the exact number wrong, but it was more than necessary. Katrina told me the state of New Jersey was going to electrocute her brother, but since he was so young, it decided on life without parole instead.

I was going to ask her if she had any similar problems with anger management, but didn't, figuring she had heard questions like that her whole life.

"Want to get some ice cream?" I asked.

It got to the point in my life where hearing a story like that didn't phase me. Not phasing me, however, phased me.

Mostly, though, in 2000, I stayed in Tulsa and lived off the money I made in 1999. The Comedy Car, the 1985 Mazda, lingered as long as it could, but then one day, on my way to meet an Indian girl for croissants, it seized up and died.

Ed, who had four cars, sold me his 1984 Toyota Tercel for the exorbitant price of $465. I told him a good uncle would have given me the fucking thing; he said a good nephew wouldn't have asked him to give up his favorite car. Still, out of the goodness of his heart (and maybe a little guilt), I got it. It may have also helped that Anita told him, "Get that piece of shit out of my driveway . . . and take the car, too."

So, there I was in 1999, 42 years old, having to replace my 1985 subcompact with a 1984 subcompact. If it weren't so funny, it would have been pathetic.

No, it was pathetic.

#!!°?)*%#*!( • ?#

In the mid '80s, I wrote book reviews for *The Tulsa World*; I also found out this year that my editor, Ken Jackson, died.

I never got paid for writing a single review; I only got to keep the books I read.

"And you should be damn happy I'm giving you those," he told me once.

I remember that gruffness. And his cough. It was the cough of two men. Robust, unapologetic, full of phlegm, it reverberated through the newsroom like a siren. And every cough sounded like it could be his last. Those coughs brought up the residue of too many cigarettes, too much whiskey, too many memories of too many women, and too many arguments with too many spineless editors, lazy reporters, and unreliable sources. Ken was stubborn, cranky, loyal, and knew it. He was a self-conscious curmudgeon, but the genuine kind.

"Who am I to review books? I haven't had anything published," I mentioned once.

"What are you talking about?" he asked through a cloud of cigarette smoke.

"Who says I'm qualified to comment on other people's work?"

"I say. And I'm the editor."

He died in a veterans' hospital, which, even though he was proud of being in the service, was probably the last place he wanted to be when it happened. I'm sure he would have preferred a newsroom ... or a bar. It had been more than five years since we talked, so I have no idea how bad the cough got, or what happened to the old Underwood typewriter on which he used to write his columns, or, whether Angie, his wife, whom he revered, sat by his bed and read his novel *Necessary* to him when he was too weak to do so himself. I'm sure he knew every word of it. When *Necessary* was first published, all his writers wanted to review it, but he decided, somewhat immodestly, to do it himself. "Not a great read," he said of his own work in his next column, "but a good one."

He was wrong; it was better than that.

I remember coming in to his office with my reviews neatly typed, sitting across his desk, and watching him edit them with the grace of a Doberman tearing into a half-pound package of ground chuck. If some piece was too long, he'd usually cut it from the bottom up. He said that the only thing to do with most of modifiers I used in a particular review was to take them out ... and shoot them.

Once, he got me a job doing stand-up at a reporter's retreat. When the organizer called and asked what my specialty was and what I would be speaking on, Ken replied, "Specialty? Nothing. He won't be speaking on anything. He's a comic."

#!!°?)*%#*!(•?#

When I returned from the Bahamas in April, I worked a week at the Tulsa club, and saw my name on the billboard as *Berry* Friedman.

*My ex-wife, who works at the club as marketing director—because apparently there are no other jobs in Tulsa where she can annoy me this much—had my name spelled incorrectly on the sign out front. Instead of it reading B-A-R-R-Y, it read FUCKHEAD, and I thought, okay, too much of a coincidence. One or two letters maybe . . .*

Work dried up the rest of that spring and summer. I went to Reno and Princeton for Catch a Rising Star, worked Don's club in Houston, but other than a few one-nighters, there wasn't much until that Corpus Christi cruise. And, since I was 43 at the time and the prospect of being that 50-year old with the bad toupee in some lounge at some Holiday Inn becoming a distinct possibility, I started looking for real work.

I knew the program director at the local public radio station and showed her some of the essays from this book, which she agreed to allow me to read on the air. She also told me a local arts magazine in Tulsa was looking for an assistant editor on a part-time basis. Neither job paid much, but it did, as my father used to tell me about work in general, give me some place to go every day. For the magazine, I wrote stories on obscure Celtic bands, a feature on Frank Sinatra, Jr., and an interview with the two guys from *Greater Tuna*. For the audio essays, I talked of my mother, Claudia, and all the pierced and damaged women I met on the road. I had to do some editing on the specificity of Cinnamon's pierced vagina and Star's D&C, but other than that, the producers kept the pieces intact. As I'm a big fan of Andrei Codrescu, I tried doing my essays with a Romanian accent, but I couldn't pull it off without sounding like Boris from the old *Rocky and Bullwinkle* cartoons.

In April, on the anniversary of my mom's death, my sister's husband, Scott, left her for the married pizza delivery woman. On the plus side, Scott was so racked with guilt over leaving Susan, he gave her almost $3,000 per month in alimony and child support. I'm sure Jane wishes I were so racked. I saw my dad as much as possible. I'd visit him in south Jersey, go to casinos with him and play keno while he played craps, and then go to diners with him and watch him flirt with waitresses 40 years younger than he. (I figured I was not the best person to give him advice on dating women his own age.) I invited him to Reno, where he won over $3,000, and where we ran into an old girlfriend of mine who wanted to come to the show. When I told her it wasn't a good idea, she left, saying something about just wanting to be friends. It reminded me of a joke I heard a comedian do about his ex-girlfriend. "She wanted to know why we couldn't be friends, and I told her, 'Because one of the friends still wants to fuck the other friend.'"

When I told my dad what my ex-girlfriend wanted, he said, "Barry, what do these girls think? They can get the perks of you being a comic without some investment on their part? Hey, it's like gambling: if you want a comp, you got to put time in at the tables."

*I don't gamble, myself. I mean I play Keno. If you don't know how to play Keno, I'll describe it to you this way: walk up to a stranger, give 'im fifty bucks and keep walking. It's the same sensation as actually playing the game. You've got a better chance of getting a hickey from Mother Teresa than you do winning this game. I play video Keno, which is where you mark your numbers on a computer screen, and then the computer picks the ones you didn't. It works out very well for the hotel.*

For my dad's 74th birthday, I invited him to Oklahoma for a Tulsa Opera production of *Turandot*. That's when he told me he was dating a girl who wanted him to meet her parents.

"Dad, you shouldn't be dating women who still have parents."

*I took my dad to Vegas and we were standing by an elevator when a showgirl walked by. The girl had hair piled high, breast cones, heavy make-up, and looked very much like a tramp. My father looked at her and said to nobody in particular, "Oh, to be sixty again."*

In January, a few days after I returned from Reno, Jane called to tell me she had found a list in Paul's wallet, reminding him to get a scale, beer, crank, the drug Ecstasy, and, surprisingly, clean the attic. Later

that day, he admitted that he was drinking, smoking (dope and cigarettes), but he was just a normal teenager. Jane and I, who couldn't
agree on whether or not the sun was shining most days, didn't agree on
the severity of this either, even when he went to the Tulsa Gun and
Knife Show and bought a stun gun and a knife. The gun I wouldn't see;
I think I met the knife, though.

The facts are that he was thrown out of school a few weeks later, not
for the drinking, but, ironically, for not attending. "But he doesn't want
to come anyway," I told the principal. "Now you're saying he can't.
That's not a punishment; that's a reward." How extensive his drug use
was I never really knew. I took him for a drug test once and while he
tested positive for pot, the rest of the result was inconclusive.

What was almost as disturbing was finding out how inconsequen-
tial I had become in his life. Maybe it was the time I spent away; maybe
it was the fact that I was a comedian; maybe it was my own lack of
resolve, but I discovered that I had no credibility and no effect.
Whatever special bond I thought we had from the trips through Kansas
and Missouri, the late night stories as he lay on one side of me in various king-sized beds, and the drives in the comedy car while we searched
beneath seats for enough money to buy a hamburger wasn't enough to
matter. I was, and this shouldn't have surprised me, anecdotal. He was
in a car accident a few days after Jane found the list (he wasn't hurt),
and when I was driving him home, waxing poetically about school and
drugs and love for a son, he said, "Listen, I don't live with you. You're
not my custodial parent, so don't tell me what to do. I don't have to listen to you. You can go fuck yourself."

I hit him somewhere between that and when he told me to just go
back to Vegas and sleep with young girls. It wasn't a punch as much as
it was a slap to the side of his head. His head snapped back more out of
surprise than force. I had never done anything like that before; I could-
n't remember the last time I even yelled at him. When we got home, I
gave him some ice to put on his eye, but he threw it back at me. The next

day, I told him that as long as he was going to continue drinking, not going to school and smoking dope, we were done. No more comedy trips, no more 1PM breakfasts of scrambled eggs and Coke, no more conversations about girls on roller coasters. It was time for me to be a father, I congratulated myself for saying. And that meant no more nickel poker games with waitresses in Vegas. I told him that someday I could imagine walking into an Italian restaurant he owned and seeing him in a tuxedo, greeting guests, and also told him I could imagine walking into a county jail and seeing him in an orange jumpsuit, wearing ankle cuffs. When he was ready for some help, I would give it to him; when he was ready to make an effort, I would help him. If he wanted to get off drugs or stop drinking, I'd find a place to take him.

He didn't laugh in my face at that moment, but Jane told me he did later. He also told Jane that I was a hypocrite for trying to be strict when for years I was a joke. And he was right. Still, consistency in parenting is overrated—especially when what you're doing is wrong. All this happened in February of 2000, and unless you count the time he pulled his knife out of his pocket and told me to *fuck off*, we didn't talk.

I wrote letters though.

*Paul, I want you to remember something: I love you.*

*Whether you smoke dope or buy stun guns, graduate from high school or get sent to prison, steal money from your mom or tell your friends I'm an asshole, I will always love you.*

*But remember this too: I won't always like you.*

*What you're doing now with your life is wrong. Period. It's dangerous. It's hurtful. It's self-destructive. And I won't be a part of it.*

*That's why you and I don't take drives in the "Lexus," or plan trips to Vegas, or sit at Charleston's* [a local restaurant] *and eat fries with bacon and cheese and ranch dressing.*

*Maybe, for you, it's a good deal. Maybe, on balance, you're okay with how things turned out; how you turned out. But should you wake up some morning, scared and lost and feel that maybe you don't have all the answers, you call me; you come over. I'll help you. I may not be your friend anymore, Paul, but I am your father.*

*Someday I'd like to tell you what that kind of love is about.*

#!!°?)*%#*!( • ?#

I met Esperanza at a hotel that's across the street from the praying hands of Oral Roberts University. At that time, she was living with her husband and her son (from a previous relationship), one of her sisters, and her sister-in-law, both of whom worked at the hotel. Esperanza, whose English was better than my Spanish (I only knew how to say *donde esta mi puta?*), was from Columbia and quickly tired of jokes about her being the daughter of the head of a Medallin drug cartel. "Barry, you are a big pain *on* my ass," she used to say. Anyway, she didn't think much of my show (I told you the women in my life never do), but she did allow me to walk her to her car that night. She still says she doesn't know why she let me kiss her in the parking lot while she sat in her Bronco. We were together through all of 2000. I flew her down to Houston with me when I worked Don's club. Actually, that's not entirely true. Her almost ex-husband, who worked for Continental Airlines, gave her free passes to fly down there. Don was with his new wife by then, so when the four of us went to dinner, he and I pretended we didn't know as much about each other as we did.

In May, I was at the Barnes and Noble near my apartment, when I met a girl who was wearing hair extensions and sweat pants, standing by the front cash register. We wound up sitting outside by the clearance rack, drinking overpriced beverages. I found out she was the chief corporate counselor for one of the major companies in town. I thought to myself, "I just met an attorney in a bookstore. Who says I can't meet normal women?"

Ha.

Not that there was anything wrong with her—unless, of course, you count some past drug, alcohol, and sexual addiction and a family which would make the Burnhams from *American Beauty* seem like the Cleavers. Her father believed that while the Germans killed some Jews during the holocaust, it wasn't on the order of six million. Janice—that's the girl—told me that her father felt maybe a hundred or so Jews were killed, but no more.

"Aside from the physical evidence, the survivors' testimony," I said, "the confessions, the archival data, does your dad really believe the Germans would build—what, 50 concentration camps that could hold up to 8,000 prisoners—and put two Jews in each? Pretty spacious accommodations, don't you think?"

"He just thinks it's a worldwide conspiracy perpetuated by Jews to elicit sympathy."

"Like we Jews have nothing else to do with our lives but come up with conspiracies to annoy people like your father."

She kept her father and me apart as much as she could.

And remember the chemist, *Amonymous?* She called one morning and said she was thinking of me and wanted to come to Tulsa. I hadn't seen her in four years, but I had chapters in a book to fill, so I agreed. Something makes it impossible for me to let moments like these go by. She came to Tulsa, and told me that in the years since I had seen her, she had been in a car accident in Vegas and injured her neck, back and elbow; consequently, she was unable to continue working as a chemist. The bright side was she had been awarded a $300,000 settlement from her insurance company. While she was waiting for the case to settle, she had taken a job working for the gas company, where she was injured again when she fell in a hole while reading meters in a trailer park.

When she came to see me, she was again out of work, had just received the 300 grand, but was in the middle of suing the state and the trailer park, which ultimately got her an additional four hundred thousand. She was sweeter and more fragile than I remembered and didn't check on the condition of her hair as much. And, best of all, she finally took off the corduroy jacket when she came to bed.

We kept in touch for a few months after that, during which time she'd call to tell me how her recuperation was going in some detail—even down to the number of clots she was passing.

Kurt Vonnegut's son, Mark, wrote a book about going insane, and in it, he concluded that even knowing the craziness was happening didn't prevent it from happening.

I had heard that Paul was back in school, so I went to Mario's Pizza, a place he was now working, to tell him that if that was the case, and, according to his mother anyway, not on drugs, we should talk. I went to the kitchen preparation area. He pulled out a knife from his pocket but didn't dislodge the blade.

"Fuck you," he said.

I followed him into the serving area.

"Look, your mother tells me you're back in school and not doing drugs, and that's good." (At this moment, he looked in my eyes and I saw they were red, dilated, and dazed.) I continued anyway. "If that's true—and remember that's why I told you I wasn't going to be a part of your life—we now have some things we can work out."

"Why don't you write another letter, you fucking wimp?"

So much for the power of rhetoric.

At this moment, the thought of throwing him into the pots and pans crossed my mind, but it wasn't my kitchen. I left Mario's with the thought that Paul was not accepting an apology I wasn't giving.

Later that evening, with Esperanza and me lying on the bed, talking about children, responsibility, and non-custodial parenting, the phone rang. I didn't answer it, but after Esperanza left, I played back the message, and found—no, not Paul—but *Amonymous*.

"Uh, Barry, some really, really bad things have happened today and

I need to talk to you. Call me anytime."

When I called back, she told me that she had started dating her old fiancé again, and, again, they decided to get married. (So far, so good.) Unfortunately, the guy was into drugs and alcohol, and when *Amonymous* asked him to quit, he said okay to the drugs, but wouldn't agree to give up drinking. She then gave him back his engagement ring and went home. Here's where the story gets interesting.

"You know how much I've always wanted to get my belly-button pierced," she said (I did?), "so I figured how hard could it be. I took out a syringe, filled it with Novocain, which I had from my back surgery, and gave myself a shot in the stomach. I then thought I'd play a stupid trick on my ex-fiancé, so I called him and told him that I was going to kill myself, and that I had already injected myself with a lethal dose of amphetamines, and said he was to blame. And then I hung up and went to take a shower."

Apparently, the boyfriend then called the fire department and police, who came to the door, and, after knocking repeatedly, broke it down, and found the syringe that she had left on the kitchen table. Hearing the commotion, *Amonymous* quickly grabbed a towel, threw on some clothes, got dressed, and climbed through a back window. She says she hid in a "crick" while the police searched the house. She was waiting for them to return when she called me.

In the middle of all this, Esperanza called to tell me she had secretly read the parts of this book about my sleeping with the lawyer and the chemist and didn't want to see me anymore.

"I'll call you right back," I said.

I hate call waiting sometimes; I clicked back.

*Amonymous* then went on to say she wasn't eating well, had lost weight, was going to the hospital if she passed one more clot, and was really depressed because the government had decided not to approve disability payments for her fall in the hole.

"Okay," I said, "Anything else?"

Ten minutes later Esperanza came over and told me that she could forgive me. I was happy, relieved, but so afraid someone else might call, I turned off the ringer.

#!!°?)*%#*!( • ?#

The next morning...

With Esperanza in the shower, I checked to see if anyone had called. Bingo!

"Hi, sweetie, it's Janice. Listen: remember those books I gave you on drug and alcohol addiction when you were worried about Paul? Remember that list of phone numbers I gave you of counselors, interventionists, and treatment centers? Well, I need all that stuff back as soon as you can bring them. I am checking myself into a treatment facility in Idaho and I need some of that information."

I then went into the bathroom and said to Esperanza, who was still showering, "I need to go out for an hour or so. I'll be right back."

I really needed one of Don's *Get Out of Jail Free* cards at this point.

I drove to Janice's mother's house, and found the mother, father, grandmother, and Janice's car in the driveway. (Her father, after seeing the old Toyota, once asked Janice what kind of man would have so little respect for himself that he'd drive such a car? I believe it's the same question Anita used to ask Ed.) Grandma opened the door, asked who I was, what I want, and how do I know Janice. I mumbled something about being asked to return some material, and am told, "She's in the shower." I gave Eva Braun the stuff and left.

Surprisingly, when I got back to the apartment, Esperanza was still there.

I then got an e-mail from Janice a few days later that read: "I'm in Idaho. Thanks for the books." She wrote to tell me that she was in treatment for taking too many pills and drinking too much alcohol. She wound up in the emergency room in Tulsa, where they pumped her stomach, and suggested—*suggested*—she get some help. She wrote again a few weeks later and said that her counselor, who specialized in behavioral matters, said he had never met a woman who was so addicted to sex.

"I hope you enjoyed being a part of my sickness." she called to say.

"Very much," I said. "I'm glad I could do my part."

#!!°?)*%#*!( • ?#

Even after my fight with Paul at Mario's, I kept going back. He wouldn't talk to me; I wouldn't talk to him. I went, in part, just to see him. The only acknowledgment I got out of him is when he tapped the bottom of the pizza pan to let me know it was hot.

He did that with everyone.

Mario, and there really is one, came from the Bronx with his wife and children and opened an original New York style pizza place right near the interstate that ran through Tulsa. Up until that time, the pizza in Tulsa had a warm cardboard and ketchup taste and feel, so I was always thankful Mario picked Tulsa and not Wichita to bring his genius.

I remember when Nina was too small to see over the counter, the guys who made the pizza gave her strips of dough, which she'd make into strange looking pies and weird kinds of animals. I told Jane, during the divorce, that she could have the house, the furniture, and whatever bank accounts we had, as long as I got Mario's. After the divorce, Paul, Nina and I would go to Mario's every Friday night. Nobody else was allowed to come. It was a routine in a family that didn't have many.

When Paul was twelve, I got him a job working there. It was against every child labor law in Oklahoma, but he wanted to work, and Mike, who now owned the place, said he'd look after him. Through the years, Mike must have fired Paul seven times, but always hired him back. When Paul first started, he'd work in the back kitchen, doing dishes, rolling meatballs, cleaning the dough machine, but then, eventually, he moved up front as an oven man and had the responsibility of turning the pizzas, adding mozzarella cheese to the meatball sandwiches, and boxing up to go. After Paul started working, Nina and I would go there for dinner by ourselves, eat Club Crackers before our meals arrived, and make funny faces at him while he was on the phone taking an order or cashing out the register. He'd always make sure my meatball sandwich and her calzone were the biggest things in the oven. Sometimes, on nights other than Fridays, I'd bring dates to the restaurant, and I'd watch Paul's expression. When he approved of the girl, he'd give me the thumbs up when she wasn't looking; when he didn't, he'd raise his eyebrows and give me the thumbs down sign when he'd spot some imperfection in her. The inside of Mario's is visible from the parking lot, so often I'd park in front and be able to see who was working behind the counter. I'd see Paul before he saw me, and in those moments, as I walked in to the restaurant, I'd think how, even if I didn't know him, I'd like to have a son like this.

Once inside, to the right, were five tables with vinyl red chairs, some torn, some not. Mounted on the wall, to the far right, was a television, usually turned to CNN during the day and ESPN at night. Next to the television was an air conditioner, painted white, embedded in the wall, which worked sporadically. Straight in from the door were more tables to the left, and farther down, the soda machine and cash register were to the right.

But it was the kitchen, especially that area between the back prep area and the counter, where I'd see Paul standing, either by the phone taking an order, or by the oven, checking the underside of a pizza when I walked in.

This was all before the craziness of this last year, but I still think of it whenever I walk in to the restaurant. Paul has a full head of blonde hair when's he's not dyeing it black or brown or cutting it in some ridiculous style. For many years, he had the requisite acne and, unlike me when I was a teenager, the kind of kid who looked good walking around without a shirt. When he'd see me, he'd wave. It wasn't a big wave; it started at his waist and made it to his chest, but never got any higher. He'd stop himself—out of embarrassment, I guess. But before he recovered that glazed, half-drunk look he worked so hard to perfect, he would be standing there with his hand open and this stupid, beautiful grin. In that moment, I could still see a little boy—my little boy. Through the people waiting to order, the pie rack where the sliced pies sat; through the people who worked there: Mike, Nick, Rob, Janet, Reynaldo, the tall, heavy Spanish kid who knew no English, there was just Paul and me. It was as if, at that moment, we were the only two people in the restaurant, the only two people in the world. There were no Miss America pageant winners, no German girls with personality disorders and scarred wrists, no breast-to-bone cancer victims lying in your mom's body, no girls who couldn't pronounce *anonymous*, no comedy disappointments, no unhappy housewives in southern California or misunderstood Vegas cocktail waitresses with interracial children, no Steve, no married Columbian girls with free airline passes, no jokes about Potsie or Jane or Bob, no tiny dancers in shitty clubs off Nebraska interstates, no pierced genitalia, no buffets in Vegas, no hair loss, no phone sex with women I just met, no book... nothing.

I still eat at Mario's, but it's more about the food now. Nina's too old to be playing with dough anymore and, besides, she's got friends who don't understand the importance of pizza generally and pizza at this place specifically, so she doesn't come with me as much as she used to. Paul's going to be 18 soon, and even though another gangly kid with acne and attitude stands where he used to, I still think of his wave when I walk inside. In that one moment, he is three years old again, lying on his stomach in his grandmother's living room, emptying out a box of 64 crayons, trying to find just the right yellow for *Curious George*; he's five, wearing batman pajamas, as he sits on my lap, sneering like an evil villain with his arms spread apart; he's eight, standing in a blue tank top with his sister and his mother as I try to take his picture and get him to smile; and he's ten, waiting in bed for me to tell him a story.

## CHAPTER 19

# Always one moment

nd then a funny thing happened on my way out of comedy: I didn't leave. I got another week in Princeton, another one in Houston, two weeks in the Tulsa club my ex-wife was now marketing, a cruise from Miami to San Juan, another New Year's date in Reno, Nevada, a week at a new club at the Excalibur in Vegas.

There's that scene in *Godfather Part III* where Michael Corleone is standing in the kitchen after escaping death, surrounded by his family, and says to everyone, "Just when I thought I was out, they pull me back in."

Comedy does that to me.

It never seems to let go.

I wish I could end this, though, by telling you about how I got my sitcom on FOX, about how I got the big break in the Schwarzenegger film, or how I opened my one man show on Broadway.

But none of that happened.

This book probably should have been written by someone like Drew Carey or Ray Romano. They—and you—know how their story ends: they make it. And a happy ending changes the point of a story.

It would be nice to have a story like that—nice to have one about syndication rights and back-end deals and hosting award shows; unfortunately, my story may end in that central Florida Holiday Inn lounge. (The toupee I will refuse to wear, though.)

Sitting on that cruise from Miami to San Juan one night, I found myself playing hide-and-go-seek with a three-year-old girl who had wandered on stage the previous evening. As she hid behind her chair from across the dining room, I covered my eyes with three fingers, pretending not to see her. She laughed and then came over and gave me some bubble gum. I knew comedy was never going to be what I wanted it to be; still, I enjoyed and missed what it had become.

I thought I was tired of it; I wasn't.

Kenny Rogerson, the comic I played nickel Keno with in Las Vegas, said the best thing about our job was that we got to hang out with the funniest people in America on a daily basis.

Ultimately, for me, comedy wasn't just about the laughs. It was the sight of all those mile markers on the Kansas interstates; the arriving at airports and waiting in baggage claim for someone to arrive from the club who almost never does; the potted plants in club lobbies that all looked the same; the lone microphone in a stand against a brick wall; the waitresses in their beige shorts and t-shirts; the radio interviews at 6AM with jocks who laugh too much and speak too loud; the redundant smell of smoke and cologne and hair spray and sex; the 4AM hamburgers from *Whataburger* when nothing else was open; the calls to agents who didn't call back; the angry, disappointed girlfriends back home who were worrying about my infidelity and their futures; and the new jokes scribbled on the backs of envelopes and business cards and parking tickets.

In comedy, you're always one booking away from two weeks of work in the Bahamas, one phone call away from a young girl with a heart problem telling you that you'll be on *Letterman*, one look away from seeing the smiles of a mom and her disabled daughter, and one show away from standing on stage and being reminded that there's no other place in the world to be.

Always one moment away from caring again.